Discover Ireland

A Comprehensive Guide to the Emerald Isle's Wonders and Traditions

Mary S. Marshall

Table of Content

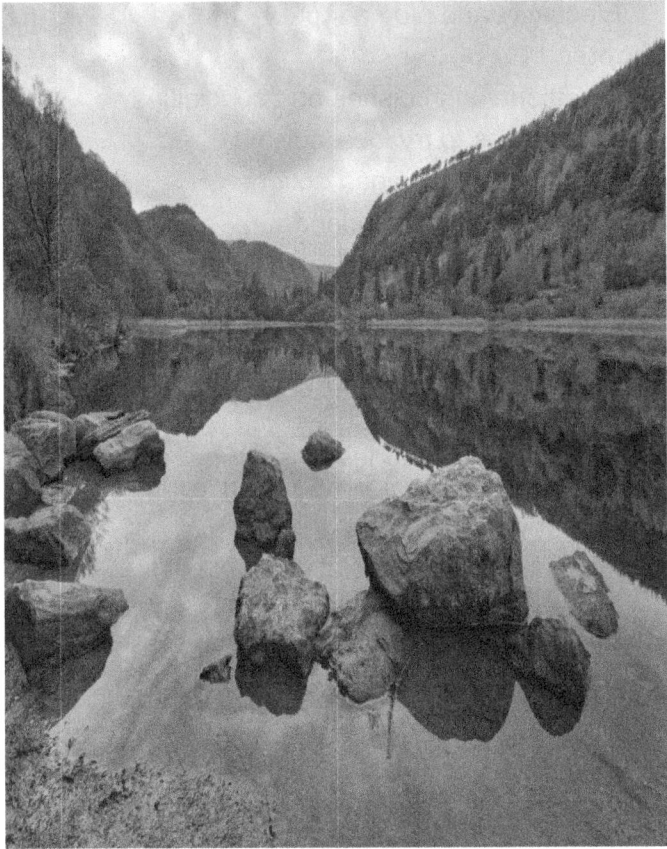

Chapter 1: Introduction to Ireland

Overview of Ireland

Ireland, known as the Emerald Isle for its lavish green scenes, is a spellbinding nation saturated with history, culture, and regular excellence. Situated in the North Atlantic, Ireland is the third-biggest island in Europe, containing the Republic of Ireland and Northern Ireland. The island is prestigious for its sensational shorelines, moving slopes, and pleasant open country, making it a heaven for nature sweethearts and outside fans.

The country's rich history goes back millennia, with proof of human settlement dating all the way back to 8000 BC. Ireland is known for its old Celtic legacy, reflected in its language, music, and workmanship. The nation has areas of strength for a custom, with renowned creators like James Joyce, W.B. Yeats, and Oscar Wilde hailing from its shores.

Ireland's dynamic culture is likewise obvious in its music and dance, with customary Irish music highlighting instruments like the fiddle, woodwind, and bodhrán. Irish dancing, with its speedy footwork and vivacious rhythms, is likewise a valued piece of the country's social legacy.

Notwithstanding its social extravagance, Ireland is likewise home to dazzling regular scenes, including rough shorelines, verdant valleys, and transcending mountains. The country's most well-known normal fascination is the Precipices of Moher, which rise grandly from the Atlantic Sea, offering stunning perspectives.

Generally, Ireland's appeal lies in its exceptional mix of history, culture, and regular magnificence, making it an enamoring objective for voyagers looking for an important encounter.

Geography and Climate

Ireland's geology and environment assume a critical role in molding the nation's scenes, verdure, fauna, and, by and large, lifestyle. Arranged in the North Atlantic Sea, Ireland is an island situated toward the northwest of mainland Europe, isolated by the Irish Ocean. It is the third-biggest island in Europe, covering an area of roughly 84,421 square kilometers.

The island's geography is described by rich green open country, moving slopes, and waterfront precipices, earning it the epithet "Emerald Isle." Ireland is likewise home to a few streams and lakes, with the Shannon Waterway being the longest waterway on the island.

The environment in Ireland is calm and oceanic, portrayed by gentle winters and cool summers. The Atlantic Sea moderately affects the environment, prompting somewhat stable temperatures consistently. Notwithstanding, the weather conditions can be altered with successive precipitation and overcast skies.

The western parts of Ireland, especially along the Atlantic coast, will generally get higher precipitation sums because of the predominant westerly breezes. The east coast, then again, will in general be drier. Snow is generally uncommon in Ireland, especially in seaside regions, yet it can happen throughout the cold weather months, particularly in higher rises.

Generally speaking, Ireland's geology and environment add to its staggering natural excellence and different biological systems. The nation's scenes are described by verdant fields, rough shorelines, and rich timberlands, making it a sanctuary for outside fans and nature sweethearts.

Best Times to Visit

The best opportunity to visit Ireland generally depends on your inclinations for climate, exercises, and groups. Ireland has a calm oceanic environment, and that implies it encounters gentle temperatures and precipitation over time. In any case, there are particular seasons that can influence the general insight of your excursion.

The most well-known chance to visit Ireland is during the mid-year stretches of June to August. During this time, the weather conditions are moderately gentle, with normal temperatures going from 15°C to 20°C (59°F to 68°F). This is likewise the most active time for the travel industry, so famous attractions and facilities might be more packed. Nonetheless, the long days take into consideration a lot of sunlight hours to investigate the staggering scenes and lively urban communities.

Spring (Walk to May) and fall (September to November) are likewise great times to visit Ireland. During these seasons, the weather conditions are as gentle as ever, and the field is flooded with lively varieties. Spring is especially gorgeous as the blossoms begin to sprout and the scenes wake up with new developments. Fall is an extraordinary opportunity to visit for those keen on climbing and outside exercises, as the weather conditions are as yet charming and the groups are more slender than in the summer.

Winter (December to February) is the calmest opportunity to visit Ireland, with fewer vacationers and lower costs. Notwithstanding, the weather conditions can be cold and wet, with temperatures averaging around 4°C to 8°C (39°F to 46°F). Regardless of the climate, winter can be a mystical opportunity to visit, particularly around Christmas when the urban communities are designed with happy lights and markets.

Taking everything into account, the best chance to visit Ireland relies upon your inclinations for climate and groups. Assuming you favor gentle temperatures and long days, summer is the best time to visit. Notwithstanding, in the event that you favor calmer environmental elements and wouldn't fret about a cooler climate, spring and pre-winter can likewise be great times to encounter the magnificence of Ireland.

Chapter 2: Trip Preparation

Planning Your Trip

Set a Budget: Decide the amount you can bear to spend on your outing, including transportation, convenience, dinners, exercises, and gifts. This will assist you in focusing on your costs and abstaining from overspending.

Choose the Ideal Opportunity to Visit: Think about the climate, swarms, and your own inclinations while picking the best chance to visit Ireland. Summer (June to August) is the most well-known time, yet spring (Walk to May) and pre-winter (September to November) can likewise be wonderful and less swarmed.

Book Flights: Search for trips to Ireland well ahead of time to get the best arrangements. Think about flying into Dublin Air Terminal, Shannon Air

Terminal, or Plug Air Terminal, contingent upon your schedule.

Apply for a Visa: Check in the event that you really want a visa to enter Ireland and apply for one if vital. Permit a lot of time for the visa application process, as it can take a little while.

"Pack Wisely": Ireland's weather conditions can be eccentric, so pack layers and waterproof clothing. Remember basics like a movement connector, toiletries, and any medications you might require.

Plan Your Itinerary: Explore the attractions and exercises you need to encounter in Ireland and make a harsh schedule. Be adaptable and permit time for unconstrained disclosures.

Book Accommodation: Exploration and book convenience ahead of time, particularly during top travel seasons. Consider remaining in lodgings, guesthouses, B&Bs, or self-catering cabins, contingent upon your inclinations and spending plan.

Arrange Transportation: Conclude how you will get around Ireland, whether by rental vehicle, public transportation, or directed visits. Book transportation ahead of time to get the best rates and accessibility.

Purchase Travel Insurance: Consider buying venture-out protection to safeguard yourself against unanticipated conditions like excursion undoings, health-related crises, or lost gear.

Learn About the Neighborhood Culture: Dive more deeply into Irish traditions, manners, and language. Realizing a couple of fundamental Irish expressions can upgrade your experience and help you recognize the neighborhood culture.

Budget for Exercises and Dining: Plan for extra costs, for example, extra charges for attractions, dinners, and gifts. Search for limits or exceptional proposals to get a good deal on exercises and feasting.

Stay Informed About Movement Advisories: Check for any tourism warnings or security cautions for Ireland before you travel. Remain informed about nearby circumstances and adhere to any rules or suggestions.

By following these means and preparing, you can guarantee a paramount and charming outing to Ireland.

Visa Requirements

Without   visa   Travel:
   - Residents of the European Association (EU), European Financial Region (EEA), and Switzerland needn't bother with a visa to visit Ireland. They are allowed to venture out to Ireland for the travel industry or business purposes for stays of as long as   90   days.
   - Residents of specific nations, including the US, Canada, Australia, and New Zealand, can likewise visit Ireland sans visa for the travel industry or business purposes for stays of as long as 90 days. This is important for Ireland's visa waiver program.

Short-Stay Visa (C-Type Visa):

- Assuming you are a resident of a country that isn't visa-excluded, you might have to apply for a short-stay visa (C-type visa) to visit Ireland for the travel industry, business, or seeing loved ones.

- The short-stay visa permits you to remain in Ireland for as long as 90 days inside a 180-day time span.

- You should apply for the visa from your nation of origin or a nation where you are a lawful occupant. Applications are made internet based through the Irish Naturalization and Migration Administration (INIS) site or through a visa application focus (VAC).

Long-Stay Visa (D-Type Visa):

- In the event that you intend to remain in Ireland for longer than 90 days, you should apply for a long-stay visa (D-type visa).

- Long-stay visas are expected for purposes, for example, study, work, joining relatives who are occupant in Ireland, or other long haul stays.

- The application cycle for a long-stay visa is more complicated and may require extra documentation, like confirmation of convenience, monetary means, and medical coverage.

Visa   Application   Process:
- To apply for a visa, you should finish a web-based application structure and submit it alongside the expected records, for example, a legitimate identification, identification estimated photos, confirmation of movement plans, and evidence of adequate assets to cover your visit.
- You may likewise have to give extra reports relying upon the inspiration of your visit. For instance, on the off chance that you are seeing family or companions, you might have to give a letter of greeting from your host.
- Visa handling times fluctuate contingent upon the nation and the season, so it is fitting to apply well ahead of your arranged travel date.

Visa   Fees:
- There is a non-refundable expense for visa applications, which shifts relying upon the sort of visa you are applying for and your identity.
- Charges are payable online at the hour of utilization and are dependent upon future

developments, so it is fitting to check the ongoing expense plan prior to applying.

Important   Considerations:

- It is essential to guarantee that your identification is substantial for no less than a half year past your expected stay in Ireland.

- You might be expected to give biometric data, like fingerprints and a computerized photo, as a feature of the visa application process.

- It is prudent to consult the authority site of the Irish Naturalization and Migration Administration (INIS) or the closest Irish international safe haven or department for the most cutting-edge data on visa necessities and application strategies.

All in all, understanding the visa necessities for visiting Ireland is fundamental for a smooth and free travel insight. By finding out more about the visa application cycle and prerequisites, you can guarantee that you have all the fundamental documentation set up before you travel.

Packing Essentials

While planning an outing to Ireland, pressing carefully can guarantee you're prepared for the country's erratic climate and different exercises. Here is an exhaustive rundown of the pressing basics for your excursion:

Clothing:

Layered Clothing: Pack lightweight, breathable layers that you can undoubtedly add or eliminate contingent upon the climate. Incorporate long-sleeved shirts, sweaters, and a waterproof coat.

Agreeable Shoes: Bring strong, waterproof strolling shoes or boots, particularly assuming that you intend to climb or investigate country regions.

Downpour Gear: A smaller umbrella and a waterproof coat or rain guard are fundamental, as downpour showers can happen much of the time.

Accessories:

Cap and Gloves: Even in summer, it's prudent to pack a cap and gloves, as temperatures can be cooler, particularly in the nights.

Scarves or Buffs: These flexible extras can provide warmth and security from wind or downpour.

Connector Plug: Ireland utilizes a Sort G electrical fitting, so carry a reasonable connector to charge your electronic gadgets.

Versatile Phone: Guarantee your telephone is opened or check with your transporter for global meandering choices. A nearby SIM card can be a smart choice for remaining associated.

Individual Cleanliness Items: Pack travel-sized toiletries like toothpaste, toothbrush, cleanser, conditioner, and cleanser.

Medications: Bring any physician-recommended drugs you expect, as well as over-the-counter solutions for normal afflictions like migraines or sensitivities.

Sunscreen: Even on shady days, UV beams can cause areas of strength. Pack a high-SPF sunscreen to safeguard your skin.

Documents:

Passport: Guarantee your identification is legitimate for somewhere around a half year past your planned stay in Ireland.

Travel Insurance: Convey a duplicate of your movement insurance contract and crisis contact data.

Schedule and Convenience Details: Print duplicates of your movement agenda and lodging reservations.

Miscellaneous Items:

Daypack: A little knapsack is helpful for road trips to convey basics like water, snacks, a guide, and a camera.

Reusable Water Bottle: Remain hydrated by topping off your jug from the many clean water sources in Ireland.

Travel Manual or Maps: While computerized choices are advantageous, an actual manual or guide can be useful, particularly in regions with restricted networks.

Travel Adapter: In the event that you intend to utilize electronic gadgets, a widespread connector can   be   helpful   for   charging.
Travel Cushion and Blanket: For long excursions or short-term visits, a movement pad and cover can make your excursion more agreeable.

By pressing these fundamentals, you'll be good to go for your excursion to Ireland, prepared to investigate its staggering scenes, energetic urban areas, and rich social legacy.

Currency and Banking

While going to Ireland, it's essential to comprehend the money utilized and the financial choices accessible to you. Here is a far-reaching manual for money and banking in Ireland:

Currency:

The cash utilized in Ireland is the Euro (€), condensed as EUR. The Euro is separated into 100 pennies, with coins accessible in groups of 1, 2, 5, 10, 20, and 50 pennies, as well as 1 and 2 Euro coins. Banknotes are accessible in sections of 5, 10, 20, 50, 100, 200, and 500 euros.

Currency   Exchange:

It's fitting to trade money before you show up in Ireland to keep away from possibly negative trade rates at air terminals or traveler regions. Significant banks and cash trade workplaces can offer this assistance.

ATMs are broadly accessible all through Ireland and are a helpful method for pulling out euros utilizing your charge or Visa. Know about any expenses your bank might charge for worldwide exchanges.

Credit   and   Charge   Cards:

Credit and check cards are generally acknowledged in Ireland, particularly in larger urban communities and traveler regions. Visa and Mastercard are the most commonly acknowledged cards, while American Express and Cafes Club might be acknowledged in certain foundations, but less ordinarily.

It's fitting to advise your bank regarding your itinerary items to keep your card from being hindered by dubious action while abroad.

Banks in Ireland are normally open Monday to Friday from 9:00 a.m. to 5:00 p.m., with certain branches shutting down for lunch between 1:00 p.m. and 2:00 p.m. A few banks may likewise be open on Saturday mornings.

ATMs:

ATMs, or "money machines," are broadly accessible in Ireland and can be found in banks, odds-and-ends shops, and traveler regions. Search for ATMs showing the Visa, Mastercard, or other applicable organization logos.

Know that a few ATMs might charge an expense for withdrawals, and your bank may likewise charge a global exchange charge.

Traveler's Checks:

Secured checks are less commonly utilized in Ireland and might be hard to cash. It's prudent to convey a limited quantity of money in euros for crises and use credit/check cards or ATMs for most exchanges.

Currency Trade Tips:

Check trade rates before you travel to guarantee you get the best incentive for your cash.

Try not to trade money at air terminals or traveler regions, as rates are frequently less great.

Use ATMs for a large portion of your money needs; however, be aware of expenses and charges.

By understanding the money and banking choices in Ireland, you can really deal with your funds and partake in a smooth and hassle-free outing.

Chapter 3: Top 5 Attractions in Ireland

The Cliffs of Moher

The Precipices of Moher are quite possibly Ireland's most notable regular fascination, famous for their staggering magnificence and emotional seaside views. Situated on the west shoreline of Ireland in Region Clare, these superb bluffs ascend to 214 meters (702 feet) over the Atlantic Sea, extending for roughly 8 kilometers (5 miles) along the shore.

Natural   Beauty:

The Bluffs of Moher are prestigious for their amazing regular magnificence, with tough precipices, ocean stacks, and caverns cut out by the persistent force of the Atlantic Sea. The precipices are layers of shale, sandstone, and siltstone, making a striking geographical development that is a demonstration of Ireland's old past.

Spectacular Views:

The precipices offer fabulous all-encompassing perspectives on the Atlantic Sea, the Aran Islands, and the Maumturks, and the Twelve Pins mountain reaches toward the north. On a sunny morning, guests can see to the extent that the mountains of Kerry toward the south and the Circle Head Promontory toward the north.

Wildlife:

The Precipices of Moher are home to a different cluster of untamed life, including seabirds like puffins, razorbills, and guillemots. The precipices are likewise an assigned Unique Insurance Region for birds, making them a well-known objective for birdwatchers.

Visitor Experience:

The Precipices of Moher Guest Experience offers guests a scope of offices and conveniences, including a guest place, display space, and shops. The guest place gives data about the set of experiences, geography, and untamed life of the precipices, as well as directed visits and varying media introductions.

Walking Trails:

The precipices are jumbled by an organization of strolling trails that permit guests to investigate the region at their own speed. The Bluffs of Moher Waterfront Walk is a famous path that runs along the precipice edge, offering staggering perspectives and photographing open doors.

O'Brien's Tower:

At the most noteworthy place of the bluffs stands O'Brien's Pinnacle, a nineteenth-century perception tower worked by nearby landowner Cornelius O'Brien. The pinnacle offers all-encompassing perspectives on the bluffs and the encompassing open country and is a famous spot for guests to take in the landscape.

Safety Precautions:

While the Precipices of Moher are a breathtaking sight, they can likewise be risky, particularly in breezy or wet circumstances. Guests are encouraged to remain in their assigned ways and try not to get excessively near the precipice edge.

Environmental   Conservation:

The Bluffs of Moher are essential for the Burren and Precipices of Moher UNESCO Worldwide Geopark, which expects to safeguard and advance the region's exceptional geographical legacy. The bluffs are likewise an assigned Unique Area of Protection, featuring their significance for biodiversity and natural preservation.

By and large, the Bluffs of Moher are a must-visit location for anybody heading out to Ireland, offering a stunning regular display that features the magnificence and force of the Irish shore.

The Ring of Kerry

The Ring of Kerry is a grand drive that circles around the Iveragh Landmass in Province Kerry, Ireland. This 179-kilometer (111-mile) course offers amazing perspectives on rough shores, immaculate seashores, pleasant towns, and staggering mountain scenes. Here is a thorough manual for investigating the Ring of Kerry:

Route and Highlights:

The Ring of Kerry starts and finishes in the town of Killarney and can be driven clockwise or counterclockwise. Along the course, you'll experience different attractions, including:

Killarney Public Park: Ireland's most seasoned public park, home to staggering lakes, timberlands, and mountains.

Muckross House: A nineteenth-century Victorian manor set in gorgeous nurseries inside Killarney Public Park.

Torc Waterfall: a beautiful cascade situated close to the N71 street, with a short strolling trail prompting the falls.

The Hole of Dunloe: A limited mountain pass that offers stunning perspectives on the encompassing scene.

Women View: A picturesque perspective that offers all-encompassing perspectives on the lakes and heaps of Killarney Public Park.

Skellig Ring: A diversion off the fundamental course that prompts the Skellig Islands, an UNESCO World Heritage Site known for their old religious settlement and staggering birdlife.

Driving Tips:

The Ring of Kerry can be limited and twisting in places, so drive cautiously and be ready to experience transport and cyclists along the course.

Permit a lot of chances to finish the drive, as you'll need to stop habitually to take in the view and investigate the attractions en route.

Think about taking a direct visit or recruiting a driver, particularly on the off chance that you're not happy driving on limited, winding streets.

Best Time to Visit:

The Ring of Kerry is wonderful all year, yet the best chance to visit is during the shoulder times of spring (Walk to May) and pre-winter (September to November), when the weather conditions are gentle and the groups are more slender.

Summer (June to August) is the most active time, with additional vacationers and higher convenience costs; however, the weather conditions are by and large hotter.

Accommodation and Dining:

There are a lot of convenience choices along the Ring of Kerry, going from lavish lodgings and guesthouses to comfortable, quaint little inns and self-cooking houses.

The course is spotted in enchanting towns where you can stop for dinner or a bite, offering a sample of customary Irish cooking.

Outdoor Activities:

The Ring of Kerry offers a lot of chances for open-air exercises, including climbing, cycling, fishing, and playing golf.

The region is additionally well known for water sports, for example, kayaking, cruising, and surfing, particularly along the shoreline.

Cultural and authentic sites:

The Ring of Kerry is saturated with history and culture, with various archeological destinations, old remains, and memorable structures to investigate.

Make certain to visit the Kerry Swamp Town Gallery, which offers a brief look into conventional Irish country life.

Environmental Conservation:

The Ring of Kerry is essential for the Wild Atlantic Way, a travel industry drive that advances and supports the travel industry along the western bank of   Ireland.

Guests are urged to regard the climate and leave no follow while investigating the region.

In general, the Ring of Kerry is a must-visit objective for anybody venturing out to Ireland, offering a beautiful drive through a portion of the nation's most shocking scenes and attractions. Whether you decide to drive the course yourself or take a directed visit, you're certain to be dazzled by the magnificence and appeal of this notorious Irish objective.

Giant's Causeway

The Monster's Highway is a one-of-a kind and shocking topographical development situated on the upper east bank of Northern Ireland. This UNESCO World Heritage Site is famous for its hexagonal basalt segments, which were framed by volcanic action a long period of time ago. Here is an extensive manual for investigating the Goliath's

Highway:

Formation and Geology:

The Goliath's Boulevard was constructed quite a while ago during a time of extraordinary volcanic movement. Magma from volcanic emissions cooled quickly when it came into contact with the virus water of the North Atlantic, bringing about the development of the trademark hexagonal basalt segments.

The sections are generally hexagonal in shape, although some have fewer or more sides. The tallest sections arrive at levels of up to 12 meters (39 feet).

Legends and Folklore:

As indicated by Irish folklore, the Goliath's Highway was worked by the monster Finn McCool, who was tested to a battle by the Scottish goliath Benandonner. Finn fabricated the interstate so they could meet; however, after seeing the size of Benandonner, he camouflaged himself as a child. At the point when Benandonner saw the size of the "child," he escaped back to Scotland, annihilating the boulevard behind him.

The Monster's Highway is one of Northern Ireland's most famous vacation destinations, drawing guests from around the world to wonder about its remarkable magnificence.

The site includes a guest place with displays on the topography and history of the interstate, as well as a bistro and gift shop.

Guests can investigate the basalt sections by strolling along assigned trails and flights of stairs that lead down to the shore. The site offers staggering perspectives on the North Atlantic Sea and the encompassing precipices.

Walking   Trails:

Notwithstanding the fundamental site of the Goliath's Highway, there are a few strolling trails in the space that offer beautiful perspectives on the shoreline and encompassing open country. The Thoroughfare Coast Way is a significant-distance strolling trail that follows the coast from the Goliath's Highway to the town of Ballycastle, passing by some of Northern Ireland's most lovely beachfront views.

Wildlife:

The Goliath's Highway is home to an assortment of natural life, including seabirds like fulmars, razorbills, and guillemots. The region is additionally known for its different vegetation, including uncommon species that flourish in the one-of-a-kind beachfront climate.

Environmental   Conservation:

The Monster's Highway and its encompassing region are safeguarded as a feature of the Goliath's Endlessly Boulevard Coast World Legacy Site. Preservation endeavors are progressing to safeguard the site's exceptional land elements and biodiversity.

Visitor   Tips:

To keep away from swarms, visit the Monster's Boulevard promptly in the first part of the day or later   at   night.

Wear tough footwear, as the basalt segments can be   elusive,   particularly   in   wet   climates.

Be ready for inconsistent weather patterns, as the North Atlantic coast can be blustery and stormy now and again.

The Goliath's Boulevard is a surprising regular miracle that offers guests a brief look into the world's topographical history. Whether you're keen on topography, folklore, or absolutely staggering normal scenes, the Monster's Thoroughfare is a must-visit objective in Northern Ireland.

Dublin's Trinity College and Book of Kells

Trinity School Dublin is Ireland's most seasoned and esteemed college, established in 1592 by Sovereign Elizabeth I. Situated in the core of Dublin, the college is famous for its notable grounds, scholarly greatness, and rich social legacy. One of the features of a visit to Trinity School is the Book of Kells, a flawlessly enlightened original copy tracing all the way back to the ninth century. Here is an exhaustive manual for investigating Trinity School and the Book of Kells:

History and Architecture:

Trinity School's grounds are a mix of memorable and current design, with structures dating from the eighteenth century to the present day. The grounds are known for their lovely Georgian squares, cobbled ways, and notable structures like the Old Library and the Campanile.

The Old Library is home to the Book of Kells and other interesting compositions, while the Long Room is a magnificent library corridor fixed with old books and marble busts of well-known essayists and researchers.

The Book of Kells:

The Book of Kells is an enlightened original copy of the four Good News accounts of the New Confirmation, made by priests in the mid-9th century. It is prestigious for its multifaceted calligraphy, dynamic outlines, and rich imagery.

The composition is housed in the Old Library's Depository, where guests can see a choice of pages in plain view. The Book of Kells show likewise incorporates intuitive presentations and data about the set of experiences and creation of the composition.

Visitor **Experience:**

A visit to Trinity School and the Book of Kells offers an interesting understanding of Ireland's social and strict history. The show gives a captivating look into the universe of middle-age original copy creation and the craft of enlightenment.

Guests can likewise investigate the Long Room, which houses more than 200,000 books and compositions, including an intriguing duplicate of the 1916 Declaration of the Irish Republic.

Guided **Visits** **and** **Events:**

Trinity School offers guided voyages through the grounds, including the Book of Kells show and the Old Library. These visits give itemized data about the set of experiences, engineering, and social meaning of the college.

The college likewise has had various comprehensive developments, talks, and presentations over time, exhibiting the rich social legacy of Ireland and the college.

To stay away from swarms, visit Trinity School and the Book of Kells show promptly in the first part of the day or later at night.

Wear agreeable footwear, as the grounds are enormous and require a decent amount of strolling.

Photography isn't permitted in the Kells show, so make certain to regard this standard.

Trinity School Dublin and the Book of Kells are must-visit attractions for anyone with any interest in Irish history, culture, and writing. A visit to this memorable college gives an intriguing understanding of Ireland's past and its rich social legacy.

Blarney Castle and the Blarney Stone

Malarkey Palace is a middle-aged post situated close to Stopper, Ireland, famous for its noteworthy importance and the Cajolery Stone, which is said to give the endowment of persuasiveness to the individuals who kiss it. Here is a thorough manual for investigating Blandishment Palace and the Cajolery Stone:

History and Architecture:

Cajolery Palace was influenced in the fifteenth century by the MacCarthy tradition, who were the leaders of the locale. The palace is an exemplary illustration of a medieval fortress, with an enormous stone keep, braced walls, and fortifications.

The palace's most renowned element is the Malarkey Stone, which is set in the palace's bastions and can be reached by climbing a thin flight of stairs.

The Cajolery Stone:

The Malarkey Stone is a block of limestone that is said to have been brought to Ireland from the Blessed Land by the Crusaders. As per legend, kissing the stone enriches the mouth with the endowment of expressiveness, or "the endowment of jabber."

To kiss the Malarkey Stone, guests should incline in reverse past the brink of the escarpments, clutching an iron railing for help, and kiss the stone beneath.

Visitor   Experience:

A visit to Malarkey Palace offers an interesting look into Ireland's medieval history and fables. The palace's interior includes a few rooms with memorable curiosities and decorations, providing guests with a feeling of what life resembled in a medieval   palace.

The palace's grounds are additionally worth investigating, with lovely nurseries, strolling trails, and picturesque perspectives on the encompassing open country.

Gardens   and   Grounds:

The palace's nurseries are a feature of any visit, with lavish vegetation, beautiful blossoms, and peaceful lakes. The Stone Close, an enchanted nursery situated close to the palace, is supposed to be home to pixies and other legendary animals.

The grounds likewise highlight various strolling trails that lead through lush regions and along the banks of the Stream Martin, offering pleasant perspectives on the palace and the encompassing open country.

Cultural Occasions and Activities: Malarkey Palace has various comprehensive developments and exercises consistently, including conventional music exhibitions, narrating meetings, and verifiable reenactments.

The palace likewise offers directed visits that give nitty-gritty data about the set of experiences and engineering of the fortification, as well as the legends and old stories related to the Cajolery Stone.

Visitor Tips: To stay away from swarms, visit Blandishment Palace promptly in the first part of the day or later at night.

Wear agreeable footwear, as the palace's grounds can be lopsided and bumpy.

Make certain to investigate the whole palace and grounds, as there are many unlikely treasures and beautiful spots to find.

Generally, a visit to Blandishment Palace and the Cajolery Stone is an unquestionable necessity for anybody heading out to Ireland. Whether you're keen on history, fables, or absolutely dazzling scenes, Malarkey Palace offers an essential encounter that will leave you feeling motivated and captivated.

Chapter 4: Experiences and Activities

Hiking in the Wicklow Mountains

Climbing in the Wicklow Mountains is a famous outside action that offers stunning perspectives, various scenes, and an opportunity to investigate Ireland's regular excellence. Found only south of Dublin, the Wicklow Mountains Public Park is a shelter for climbers and open-air devotees, with various paths reasonable for all degrees of involvement. Here is a far-reaching manual for climbing in the Wicklow Mountains:

Trails   and   Routes:
   The Wicklow Way is a significant-distance climbing trail that runs for 131 kilometers (81 miles) through the Wicklow Mountains, from Marlay Park in Dublin to Clonegal in Region Carlow. The path goes through different scenes, including mountains,

timberlands, and valleys, and offers dazzling perspectives on the encompassing open country.

There are additionally numerous more limited climbing trails nearby, going from simple strolls to more difficult climbs. Famous courses incorporate the Glendalough Spinc and the Luggala Circle, the two of which offer fabulous perspectives and an opportunity to investigate the mountains' extraordinary greenery.

Scenic   Highlights:

One of the features of climbing in the Wicklow Mountains is the staggering view. The mountains are home to beautiful valleys, shining lakes, and rough pinnacles, offering a lot of chances for grand photograph   stops.

Glendalough, a frigid valley with a sixth-century religious settlement, is a must-visit objective for explorers. The valley is home to two delightful lakes, encompassed by rich woodlands and transcending mountains.

Flora   and   Fauna:

The Wicklow Mountains are home to a different scope of plant and creature species, including interesting orchids, mountain rabbits, and red deer. Birdwatchers will likewise be pleased by the assortment of birdlife nearby, including peregrine hawks and brilliant falcons.

The Wicklow Mountains Public Park Guest Center, situated in Glendalough, gives data about the recreation area's set of experiences, untamed life, and climbing trails. The middle additionally offers directed strolls and instructive projects for guests.

There are a few convenience choices nearby, going from camping areas and lodgings to guesthouses and inns. It's prudent to book convenience ahead of time, particularly during the pinnacle climbing season.

Climbing in the mountains can be testing, so it's critical to be ready. Wear strong climbing boots, dress in layers, and convey a lot of water and tidbits.

Know about the atmospheric conditions, as they can change rapidly in the mountains. Check the weather conditions conjecture before you set out and be ready for downpours, wind, and haze.

It's likewise really smart to convey a guide and compass or a GPS gadget, as certain paths can be ineffectively checked.

Climbing in the Wicklow Mountains offers a novel chance to investigate Ireland's shockingly normal scenes and rich biodiversity. Whether you're an accomplished climber searching for a test or a beginner explorer hoping to investigate nature, the Wicklow Mountains have something for everybody.

Exploring ancient ruins such as Newgrange

Investigating old vestiges in Ireland, like Newgrange, offers an entrancing look into the country's rich history and ancient past. Newgrange is a Neolithic entombment hill situated in Province Meath, going back north of 5,000 years, making it more established than Stonehenge and the

Incomparable Pyramids of Giza. Here is an extensive manual for investigating old remains like Newgrange:

History and Significance:

Newgrange is essential for the Brú na Bóinne UNESCO World Legacy Site, which likewise incorporates the section burial places of Knowth and Dowt. h. These antiquated landmarks are among the main ancient locales in Europe, exhibiting the high level of compositional and designing abilities of the Neolithic nation, which assembled the m.

Newgrange is especially renowned for its colder time of year solstice peculiarity. Throughout the colder time of year solstice, a tight light emission enters the entry burial place's rooftop box and enlightens the focal chamber, denoting the resurrection of the sun and perhaps filling in as a strict or stylized importance for the Neolithic public.

Visitor Experience:

Guests to Newgrange can investigate the outside of the burial place, which includes enormous kerb stones engraved with unpredictable plans, as well as the inside, which comprises a long section prompting a focal chamber. Admission to the inside of Newgrange is confined and requires a direct visit, as the section and chamber are tight and can accommodate a few individuals all at once.

Archaeological Discoveries:

Unearthings at Newgrange have uncovered an abundance of archeological finds, including incinerated human remains, stoneware, and different relics. These disclosures have given significant insight into the strict convictions, entombment practices, and social construction of Neolithic culture.

Visitor Center and Facilities:

The Bru na Boinne Guest Center, situated close to Newgrange, gives data about the site's set of experiences, paleohistory, and importance. e. The middle likewise offers directed visits and presentations displaying antiques found at Newgrange and other close-by destinations. s. Offices at the guest place incorporate a bistro, gift shop, and stopping area. It's prudent to book directed visits ahead of time, particularly during peak travel seasons.

Environmental   Conservation:

Newgrange and the encompassing region are safeguarded as a component of the Brú na Bóinne World Legacy Site. e. Preservation endeavors are continuous to save the site's old designs as well as its common habitat and biodiversity. y.

Guests are urged to regard the site's legacy and observe assigned ways and rules to limit influence on the antiquated remnants.

Investigating old vestiges like Newgrange offers a one-of-a-kind chance to step back in time and find Ireland's old past. Whether you're keen on paleontology, history, or basically investigating old secrets, Newgrange and other ancient locales in Ireland make certain to charm and move.

Traditional music and dance performances

Customary music and dance are indispensable pieces of Irish culture, mirroring the country's rich legacy and history. From exuberant dances and reels to tormenting songs, customary Irish music has a remarkable sound that has dazzled crowds all over the planet. Essentially, Irish dance, with its unpredictable footwork and vivacious rhythms, is a lively articulation of Irish personality. Here is a thorough manual for customary music and dance exhibitions in Ireland:

Traditional   Music:
Conventional Irish music is characterized by its utilization of instruments, for example, the fiddle, tin whistle, woodwind, bodhrán (drum), and accordion. These instruments meet up to make an energetic and irresistible sound that is inseparable from Irish music.

Meetings, or casual social occasions where performers meet up to play conventional music, are a typical sight in bars and music scenes across

Ireland. These meetings are an extraordinary method for encountering conventional Irish music in a loose and casual environment.

Traditional   Dance:

Irish dance is described by its quick footwork and upstanding stance. The most popular type of Irish dance is step-moving, which is a performance that highlights mind-boggling footwork and exact developments.

One more well-known type of Irish dance is set dancing, which is acted out in gatherings and elements as a progression of steps and developments that are moved to customary Irish music.

Performance   Venues:

Conventional music and movement exhibitions can be tracked down in various scenes across Ireland, including bars, music settings, and social focuses. Numerous urban communities and towns additionally have customary live concerts and occasions.

Famous Performers:

Ireland has delivered numerous renowned customary performers and artists, including performers like The Tribal Leaders, The Dubliners, and artists like Michael Flatley and Jean Steward. These entertainers have assisted in advocating customary Irish music and dance all over the planet.

Cultural Significance:

Conventional music and dance are a significant piece of Irish culture and character, filling in as a method for commending and safeguarding Ireland's rich legacy. Numerous conventional Irish tunes and moves have been passed down through the ages, filling in as a connection to Ireland's past.

Tourist Experiences:

For vacationers visiting Ireland, customary music and dance exhibitions offer an extraordinary and essential social experience. Numerous vacation spots, for example, the Bunratty Palace and Society Park in District Clare, offer conventional music and dance exhibitions as a feature of their diversion contributions.

Guests can likewise go to conventional music meetings in bars and music scenes the nation over, submerging themselves in the enthusiastic and inviting air of Irish music and dance.

Learning   Opportunities:

For those keen on finding out about customary Irish music and dance, there are numerous valuable chances to take classes and studios in Ireland. These classes offer an opportunity to learn from experienced performers and artists and to encounter the delight of conventional Irish music and dance firsthand.

By and large, customary music and dance are dynamic articulations of Irish culture, mirroring the country's rich history and legacy. Whether you're watching a presentation in a bar or participating in a meeting, encountering customary Irish music and dance is certain to be a feature of any excursion to Ireland.

Whiskey tasting tours

Bourbon tasting visits in Ireland offer an exceptional and vivid experience for bourbon lovers and sightseers alike, giving an opportunity to find out about the set of experiences, creation, and tasting of Ireland's popular soul. From notable refineries to present-day makers, Ireland's bourbon industry has a rich and different legacy that is definitely worth investigating. Here is an extensive manual for bourbon tasting visits in Ireland:

History of Irish Whiskey:
Irish bourbon has a long and celebrated history, dating all the way back to the sixth century, when Irish priests are said to have carried the specialty of refining to Ireland. By the nineteenth century, Irish bourbon was one of the most famous spirits on the planet, known for its perfection and quality.

The Irish bourbon industry went through a decline in the twentieth century because of elements like preclusion and rivalry from different spirits. Notwithstanding, lately, there has been a resurgence of interest in Irish whiskey, with new refineries opening and old ones being resuscitated.

There are a few sorts of Irish bourbon, including single malt, single pot, mixed bourbon, and grain bourbon. Each type has its own remarkable qualities and flavor profile, contingent upon elements, for example, the fixings utilized, the refining system, and the maturing system. Single-malt bourbon is produced using 100 percent malted grain and refined in pot stills. It is known for its smooth and complex flavor profile, with notes of malt,   natural   products,   and   flavors.

Single pot still Bourbon is produced using a blend of malted and unmalted grain and is refined in pot stills. It is one of a kind in Ireland and is known for its rich and velvety surface, with notes of nuts, organic products, and flavors.

Whiskey   Tasting   Tours:

Bourbon tasting visits in Ireland offer guests an opportunity to visit refineries, find out about the bourbon-making cycle, and test an assortment of Irish bourbons. Visits are regularly driven by educated guides who can give experiences into the set of experiences and creation of Irish bourbon.

Numerous refineries offer directed visits that take guests through the refining system, from squashing and maturation to refining and maturing. Guests can likewise find out about the various sorts of Irish bourbon and how they are made.

Bourbon tasting meetings are a feature of the visit, permitting guests to test a choice of bourbons and find out about the unique flavors and smells of each. Tastings are often joined by master critiques of the Bourbons' attributes and creation techniques.

Distillery   Visits:

The absolute most well-known refineries in Ireland offer bourbon tasting visits, remembering the Old Bushmills Refinery for Northern Ireland, the Jameson Refinery in Dublin, and the Midleton Refinery in Province Plug. These refineries are famous for their excellent bourbons and their noteworthy   importance.

Refinery visits frequently incorporate a direct visit through the offices, a tasting meeting of the refinery's scope of bourbons, and the chance to buy bourbon-related keepsakes and presents.

Cultural and Social Experience:

Bourbon tasting visits in Ireland are not just about testing bourbon; they likewise offer a social experience. Guests can find out about Ireland's bourbon-making legacy, meet individual bourbon devotees, and partake in the warm cordiality of the Irish public.

Many visits additionally incorporate visits to neighborhood bars and eateries, where guests can test customary Irish dishes and appreciate unrecorded music and amusement. This is a one-of-a kind chance to encounter Irish culture and neighborliness firsthand.

Safety and Responsibility:

It's critical to drink responsibly while taking part in whiskey tasting visits. Most refineries give spittoons to guests to use during tastings, permitting them to test the bourbon without consuming huge amounts.

Guests ought to likewise sort out transportation to and from the refinery, as driving under the influence is both unlawful and risky.

In general, bourbon tasting visits in Ireland offer a remarkable and paramount experience for bourbon devotees and sightseers alike. Whether you're a carefully prepared bourbon epicurean or only inquisitive to more deeply study Irish bourbon, a bourbon tasting visit makes certain to be a feature of your outing to Ireland.

Golfing at renowned courses

Playing golf in Ireland is a top-notch insight, with the nation boasting some of the most prestigious and beautiful fairways on the planet. From joining courses along the rough shore to parkland courses set in the midst of moving green slopes, Ireland offers a different scope of hitting the fairway encounters for players, everything being equal. Here is a complete manual for playing golf at famous courses in Ireland:

"History of Golf in Ireland": Golf has a long history in Ireland, with the game considered to have been introduced to the country in the nineteenth century. The Imperial Belfast Golf Club, established in 1881, is one of the most seasoned golf clubs in Ireland and is still in activity today.

Ireland has delivered numerous extraordinary golf players throughout the long term, including significant bosses like Rory McIlroy, Padraig Harrington, and Darren Clarke, who have assisted with raising the profile of Irish golf on the global stage.

Types of Golf Courses:
Ireland is home to an assortment of fairways, including joint courses, parkland courses, and inland courses. Joint courses are situated along the coast and are described by their regular, rough territory and testing format.

Parkland courses, then again, are set inland and are known for their manicured fairways, lavish plant life, and picturesque environmental elements. Inland courses offer a more quiet and disconnected playing golf experience with fewer interruptions from the rest of the world.

Renowned Golf Courses:
Ireland is home to probably the most prestigious fairways on the planet, including: **Old Course at Ballybunion Golf Club:** Situated on the southwest bank of Ireland, Ballybunion is reliably positioned as one of the top courses on the planet. The Old Course is known for its difficult design, staggering waterfront perspectives, and normal magnificence.

Illustrious District Down Golf Club: Situated in Northern Ireland, Regal Area Down is another highest-level course known for its difficult design and amazing landscape. The course is set against the background of the Mourne Mountains and offers dazzling perspectives on the Irish Ocean.

Lahinch Golf Club: Situated on the west shore of Ireland, Lahinch is a noteworthy connections course known for its undulating fairways, testing dugouts, and dazzling perspectives on the Atlantic Sea. The course has facilitated numerous renowned competitions throughout the long term and is #1 among expert and beginner golf players alike.

Golfing Facilities:

A considerable number of Ireland's top greens offer elite offices, including practice regions, clubhouses, master shops, and eating choices. A few courses likewise offer convenience on location or in association with neighborhood lodgings, making it simple for golf players to remain and play. Golf players can likewise exploit golf bundles and visits, which consolidate rounds of golf at different courses with convenience, transportation, and different conveniences. These bundles are an extraordinary method for encountering the best that Irish golf brings to the table.

"Scenic and Normal Beauty":

One of the features of playing golf in Ireland is the dazzling normal excellence of the nation's scenery. From the rough shoreline of the Wild Atlantic Way to the moving green slopes of the Irish open country, Ireland offers probably the most beautiful and grand-hitting fairway settings on the planet. Many greens in Ireland are situated close to notable locales, palaces, and different attractions, making them ideal objections for golf players who need to consolidate their enthusiasm for the game with touring and investigation.

Golfing Occasions and Tournaments: Ireland has various lofty hitting the fairway occasions and competitions consistently, including the Irish Open and the Ryder Cup. These occasions draw in top golf players from around the world, giving prospective onlookers an opportunity to see probably the best players in real life.

In general, hitting the fairway in Ireland is a genuinely extraordinary encounter, with top-notch courses, a shocking landscape, and a rich history and legacy that make it a must-visit objective for golf lovers. Whether you're a carefully prepared golf player hoping to test your abilities on testing joint courses or an easygoing player hoping to partake in a relaxed round in the midst of wonderful environmental factors, Ireland brings something to the table for golf players of all levels and capacities.

Chapter 5: Top 5 Cities to Visit

Dublin

Dublin, the capital city of Ireland, is an energetic and dynamic city with a rich history, lively culture, and warm cordiality. From noteworthy milestones to vivacious bars, Dublin offers a different scope of attractions and encounters for guests to appreciate. Here is a far-reaching manual for investigating Dublin:

History and Landmarks: Dublin is saturated with history, with a legacy that goes back more than 1,000 years. The city is home to numerous memorable landmarks, including Dublin Palace, Christ Church Basilica, and St. Patrick's Basilica, which feature the city's rich engineering and social legacy. The city's Georgian engineering is likewise a noticeable component, with some very well-saved structures dating from the eighteenth century.

Merrion Square and Fitzwilliam Square are especially striking for their exquisite Georgian apartments and verdant parks.

Cultural   Attractions:
Dublin is a social center point, with an abundance of exhibition halls, displays, and theaters to investigate. The Public Exhibition Hall of Ireland, the Irish Historical Center of Present-Day Craftsmanship, and the Chester Beatty Library are only a couple of the city's social features. The city is likewise known for its scholarly legacy, with numerous renowned essayists and artists calling Dublin home. Guests can investigate the Dublin Journalists Exhibition Hall, take a scholarly bar crawl, or visit the origins of renowned Irish essayist James Joyce.

Shopping   and   Dining:
Dublin offers a different scope of shopping choices, from very good-quality shops to particular free stores. Grafton Road and Henry Road are well-known shopping destinations, offering everything from style and accessories to trinkets and gifts. The city is likewise famous for its culinary scene,

with a great many cafés, bistros, and diners to browse. Customary Irish bars present generous bar grub, while top-notch cafés offer connoisseur cooking made with privately obtained fixings.

Entertainment and Nightlife:

Dublin is known for its vivacious nightlife, with an abundance of bars and clubs to look over. The Sanctuary Bar region is especially famous for its cobblestone roads and dynamic climate. The city likewise has a flourishing music scene, with unrecorded music settings exhibiting everything from conventional Irish music to contemporary rock and pop. The popular Whelan's setting is a must-visit for music darlings.

Parks and Outside Spaces:

In spite of being a clamoring city, Dublin has many green spaces where guests can unwind and loosen up. Phoenix Park, quite possibly the biggest metropolitan park in Europe, is a famous destination for picnics, strolls, and bicycle rides. The Public Botanic Nurseries and St. Stephen's Green are likewise worth a visit, offering a quiet retreat from the buzzing about of the city.

Transportation and Accessibility: Dublin is all around associated with open transportation, with a broad transport and cable car network serving the city and its rural areas. The city is additionally minimal and walkable, making it simple to investigate by walking. For those hoping to investigate the past as far as possible, Dublin is an extraordinary base for roadtrips to attractions like the Bluffs of Moher, the Wicklow Mountains, and the Boyne Valley.

Dublin's rich history, lively culture, and warm friendliness make it a must-visit objective for explorers to Ireland. Whether you're investigating the city's memorable milestones, examining its culinary joys, or absorbing its energetic climate, Dublin has something for everybody to appreciate.

Galway

Galway, frequently alluded to as the "social heart of Ireland," is an energetic city situated on the west bank of Ireland. Known for its rich history, creative legacy, and enthusiastic climate, Galway offers guests an interesting mix of conventional Irish culture and present-day enchantment. Here is a complete manual for investigating Galway:

History and Landmarks:

Galway has a long and captivating history, with proof of human settlement dating back over 4,000 years. The city's middle-age past is obvious in its memorable tourist spots, including the Spanish Curve, a remnant of the city's middle-age protections, and Lynch's Palace, a sixteenth-century condo that currently houses a gallery. Eyre Square, situated in the core of the city, is a well-known get-together spot and a center of movement, with its lovely nurseries, sculptures, and verifiable importance.

Cultural Attractions:

Galway is famous for its energetic expressions and cultural scene, with an abundance of exhibitions, theaters, and execution spaces to investigate. The Galway Expressions Celebration, held yearly in July, is one of the city's most well-known and far-reaching developments, exhibiting a different scope of expression and diversion. The city is likewise known for its conventional Irish music scene, with numerous bars and settings facilitating unrecorded music meetings. The Galway Irish Gem Legacy Center is a must-visit for those keen on the city's high-quality art and customs.

Shopping and Dining: Galway offers an exceptional shopping experience, with a blend of very good-quality stores, distinctive specialty shops, and conventional business sectors. The Galway Market, held consistently, is an incredible spot to get neighborhood specialties, food, and trinkets. The city is likewise known for its culinary scene, with a great many cafés, bistros, and diners offering everything from customary Irish dishes to global cooking. The Latin Quarter is an especially famous eating destination, with its enchanting roads fixed with eateries and bars.

Entertainment and Nightlife: Galway is renowned for its lively nightlife, with plenty of bars and clubs to look over. The city's bar scene is incredible, with numerous customary Irish bars facilitating unrecorded music meetings and offering a warm and inviting climate. The Roísiún Dubh and the Galway Global Expressions Celebration are famous settings for unrecorded music and diversion, displaying a blend of neighborhood and worldwide art. y.

Outdoor   Activities:
Galway is encircled by shocking regular excellence, with the tough Connemara scene and the beautiful shoreline simply a short drive away. Outside fans can partake in a range of exercises, including climbing, cycling, fishing, and hitting the fairway. The Bluffs of Moher, perhaps Ireland's most famous regular milestone, are likewise within easy reach of Galway and make for a paramount road trip.

Transportation   and   Accessibility:
Galway is very much associated with open transportation, with normal transport and train administrations interfacing the city with different parts of Ireland. The city is likewise reduced and walkable, making it simple to investigate by

walking.

For those hoping to investigate the past as far as possible, Galway is an incredible base for road trips to attractions like the Aran Islands, Connemara Public Park, and the Burren.

Galway's special mix of history, culture, and normal excellence makes it a must-visit objective for voyagers to Ireland. Whether you're investigating the city's memorable milestones, absorbing its imaginative legacy, or partaking in its vivacious nightlife, Galway has something for everybody to appreciate.

Cork

Plug, frequently alluded to as the "genuine capital of Ireland," is a lively city situated in the southwest of Ireland. Known for its rich history, energetic social scene, and dazzling normal excellence, Plug offers guests a novel mix of customary Irish appeal and present-day refinement. Here is a complete manual for investigating Plug:

History and Landmarks:

Stopper has a long and intriguing history, with proof of human settlement dating back more than 1,000 years. The city's memorable tourist spots mirror its rich legacy, including the Stopper City Gaol, a previous jail that is presently an exhibition hall, and the Elizabeth Post, a seventeenth-century fortress that offers all-encompassing perspectives on the city.

St. Blade Barre's House of Prayer, with its shocking Gothic engineering, is another must-visit milestone that features Plug's compositional legacy.

Cultural Attractions:

Plug is eminent for its dynamic expressions and cultural scene, with an abundance of displays, theaters, and execution spaces to investigate. The Stopper Drama House is a famous scene for music, theater, and dance exhibitions, while the Crawford Workmanship Display displays a different assortment of Irish and worldwide craftsmanship. The city is additionally known for its celebrations, including the Plug Jazz Celebration and the

Stopper Midsummer Celebration, which draw in guests from around the world.

Shopping and Dining: Stopper offers a different scope of shopping choices, from top-line stores to eccentric free stores. The English Market, one of the most established city markets of its sort, is a must-visit objective for foodies, offering an extensive variety of neighborhood produce and distinctive merchandise.

The city's culinary scene is similarly noteworthy, with a large number of cafés, bistros, and diners offering everything from conventional Irish dishes to global food. The clamoring paths of the downtown area are fixed with bistros, bars, and eateries, offering different feasting choices to suit each taste and financial plan.

Entertainment and Nightlife: Plug is known for its enthusiastic nightlife, with plenty of bars and clubs to browse. The city's bar scene is unbelievable, with numerous customary Irish bars facilitating unrecorded music meetings and offering a warm and inviting air.

The Stopper Drama House and the Everyman Theater are well-known settings for unrecorded music, theater, and dance exhibitions, displaying a blend of local and global ability.

Outdoor   Activities:
Plug is encircled by staggering regular magnificence, with the tough shoreline and beautiful wide open simply a short drive away. Open-air fans can partake in a range of exercises, including climbing, cycling, fishing, and hitting the fairway.

The nearby town of Kinsale is a well-known objective for water sports fans, with its protected harbor and sandy seashores offering a range of exercises like cruising, kayaking, and windsurfing.

Transportation and Accessibility:
Stopper is very much associated with open transportation, with customary transport and train administrations interfacing the city with different parts of Ireland. The city is additionally reduced and walkable, making it simple to investigate by walking.

For those hoping to investigate the past as far as

possible, Stopper is an extraordinary base for road trips to attractions, for example, the Cajolery Palace, the Jameson Refinery in Midleton, and the Grand Ring of Kerry.

Plug's interesting mix of history, culture, and regular magnificence makes it a must-visit objective for voyagers to Ireland. Whether you're investigating the city's notable milestones, partaking in its energetic expressions and culture scene, or testing its culinary pleasures, Plug has something for everybody to appreciate.

Limerick

Limerick, situated in the midwest of Ireland, is a city saturated with history, culture, and appeal. Known for its pleasant riverside setting, middle-age engineering, and lively expressions scene, Limerick offers guests an abundance of attractions and encounters to appreciate. Here is a thorough manual for investigating Limerick:

History and Landmarks:
Limerick has a rich and celebrated history, dating back over 1,000 years. The city's notable tourist spots mirror its middle-aged past, including Ruler John's Palace, a thirteenth-century post that offers all-encompassing perspectives on the city and the Shannon Waterway. The Settlement Stone, situated on Clancy Strand, denotes where the Arrangement of Limerick was endorsed in 1691, finishing the Williamite Battle in Ireland.

Cultural Attractions:
Limerick is famous for its lively arts and culture scene, with an abundance of exhibitions, theaters, and execution spaces to investigate. The Limerick City Display of Craftsmanship displays a different assortment of Irish workmanship, while the Belltable Expressions Place has various exhibitions, presentations, and occasions. The city is likewise known for its scholarly legacy, with numerous renowned authors and writers calling Limerick home. The Honest McCourt Exhibition Hall, situated in the previous school

building of the Pulitzer Prize-winning creator, offers a captivating insight into his life and work.

Shopping and Dining: Limerick offers a different scope of shopping choices, from very good-quality shops to particular free stores. The Milk Market, situated in the downtown area, is a famous objective for foodies, offering an extensive variety of nearby produce and high-quality merchandise. The city's culinary scene is similarly great, with a large number of cafés, bistros, and restaurants offering everything from conventional Irish dishes to global cooking. The memorable roads of the downtown area are fixed with bistros, bars, and cafés, offering various feasting choices to suit each taste and financial plan.

Entertainment and Nightlife: Limerick is known for its vivacious nightlife, with plenty of bars and clubs to browse. The city's bar scene is incredible, with numerous customary Irish bars facilitating unrecorded music meetings and offering a warm and inviting climate. Dolan's Distribution Center and the College Show

Corridor are famous scenes for unrecorded music and diversion, exhibiting a blend of neighborhood and worldwide ability.

Limerick is encircled by shockingly normal excellence, with the Stream Shannon and the moving slopes of District Limerick simply a short drive away. Open-air fans can partake in a range of exercises, including climbing, cycling, fishing, and playing   golf.
The close-by towns of Adare and Newcastle West are well-known objections to outside exercises, with their pleasant open country and beguiling towns offering a tranquil retreat from the hurrying around of city life.

Transportation   and   Accessibility:
Limerick is very much associated with open transportation, with standard transport and train administrations interfacing the city with different parts of Ireland. The city is likewise minimal and walkable, making it simple to investigate by walking.
For those hoping to investigate the past as far as

possible, Limerick is an incredible base for road trips to attractions like the Bluffs of Moher, the Burren, and the Wild Atlantic Way.

Limerick's extraordinary mix of history, culture, and regular excellence makes it a must-visit objective for voyagers to Ireland. Whether you're investigating the city's noteworthy milestones, partaking in its lively expressions and culture scene, or basically loosening up by the Waterway Shannon, Limerick has something for everybody to appreciate.

Belfast

Belfast, the capital city of Northern Ireland, is a city of differences, mixing a rich modern legacy with lively expressions and culture. From noteworthy milestones to exuberant bars, Belfast offers guests a different scope of attractions and encounters to appreciate. Here is a complete manual for investigating Belfast:

History and Landmarks:
Belfast has a long and captivating history, dating back more than 1,000 years. The city's notable tourist spots mirror its modern past, including the Harland and Wolff shipyards, where the RMS Titanic was assembled. Belfast City Lobby, a staggering illustration of Florid Recovery design, is another must-visit milestone that demonstrates the city's structural legacy.

Cultural Attractions:
Belfast is prestigious for its lively arts and culture scene, with an abundance of exhibitions, theaters, and execution spaces to investigate. The Ulster Historical Center, situated in the Botanic Nurseries, boasts a different assortment of workmanship, history, and inherent sciences. The city is additionally known for its abstract legacy, with numerous popular scholars and artists calling Belfast home. The Seamus Heaney HomePlace, situated in neighboring Bellaghy, praises the life and work of the Nobel Prize-winning artist.

Shopping and Dining:
Belfast offers a different scope of shopping choices, from top-of-the line stores to particular free stores. Victoria Square, with its shocking glass vault, is a famous shopping destination, offering a blend of global brands and nearby stores. The city's culinary scene is similarly noteworthy, with a large number of cafés, bistros, and restaurants offering everything from conventional Irish dishes to global cooking. The House of God Quarter is an especially well-known eating objective, with its enthusiastic climate and diverse blend of eateries and bars.

Entertainment and Nightlife:
Belfast is known for its enthusiastic nightlife, with plenty of bars and clubs to look over. The city's bar scene is incredible, with numerous customary Irish bars facilitating unrecorded music meetings and offering a warm and inviting air. The SSE Field Belfast and the Waterfront Corridor are well-known scenes for unrecorded music and diversion, displaying a blend of nearby and worldwide ability.

Outdoor   Activities:

Belfast is encircled by dazzling normal excellence, with the beautiful Antrim Coast and the tough Mourne Mountains simply a short drive away. Open-air devotees can partake in a range of exercises, including climbing, cycling, and fishing. The nearby town of Carrickfergus is home to a very well-guarded Norman palace, while the Monster's Boulevard, an UNESCO World Heritage Site, is a must-visit objective for nature darlings.

Transportation   and   Accessibility:

Belfast is very much associated with open transportation, with ordinary transport and train administrations interfacing the city with different parts of Northern Ireland and the Republic of Ireland. The city is likewise minimal and walkable, making it simple to investigate by walking. For those hoping to investigate the past as far as possible, Belfast is an incredible base for roadtrips to attractions, for example, the Monster's Thoroughfare, the Carrick-a-Rede Rope Extension, and the Dim Supports.

Belfast's exceptional mix of history, culture, and regular magnificence makes it a must-visit objective for explorers to Northern Ireland. Whether you're investigating the city's noteworthy milestones, partaking in its energetic expressions and culture scene, or just absorbing the enthusiastic climate, Belfast has something for everybody to appreciate.

Chapter 6: Culture and Traditions

Irish folklore and mythology

Irish old stories and folklore are a necessary piece of the country's rich social legacy, well established in the old practices of the Celtic public. These stories, which went down through the ages, are a mix of history, legend, and creative mind, mirroring the convictions, values, and lifestyle of the Irish public. Here is a complete manual for Irish fables and folklore:

The Tuatha Dé Danann: As per Irish folklore, the Tuatha Dé Danann were an extraordinary race of creatures who occupied Ireland before the appearance of the Milesians, the progenitors of cutting-edge Irish individuals. They were talented in enchantment and had extraordinary information and astuteness.

The Tuatha Dé Danann were related to the components of nature and were accepted to have command over the climate, the land, and the ocean. They were likewise known for their ability to fight and were loved as divine beings and goddesses by the antiquated Celts.

The   Fianna:
The Fianna were an incredible band of champions who meandered Ireland during the hour of the Great Rulers. Driven by the unbelievable legend Fionn macintosh Cumhaill, the Fianna were known for their grit, expertise in fighting, and adherence to a   severe   code   of   honor. The stories of the Fianna are loaded with experience, sentiment, and interest and are a focal piece of Irish legend. A large number of these accounts have been passed down through oral practice and have turned into a significant piece of Ireland's social legacy.

The   Sidhe:
The Sidhe, or pixie people, are otherworldly creatures in Irish fables who are accepted to occupy the antiquated hills and slopes of Ireland.

They are known for their excellence, their mysterious powers, and their devilish nature. The Sidhe are supposed to be gatekeepers of the land and are related to both altruistic and pernicious deeds. They are frequently portrayed as either supportive or hurtful to people, contingent upon their state of mind and aims.

Mythological Creatures:

Irish folklore is rich in stories of legendary animals, including leprechauns, banshees, and selkies. These animals are frequently portrayed as strange and extraordinary, with powers and capacities beyond those of mortal creatures. Leprechauns are maybe the most popular of these animals, known for their naughty nature and their treasures that may be impossible to obtain but are still worth working for. Banshees are spirits who are said to proclaim demise with their sad cries, while selkies are seals who can shed their skin and take on human structure.

Celtic Celebrations and Traditions:

A large number of Ireland's conventional celebrations and customs are established in Celtic folklore and fables. The most renowned of these is Samhain, the antiquated Celtic celebration that marks the end of the collecting season and the start of winter. Other significant Celtic celebrations incorporate Imbolc, Beltane, and Lughnasadh, each of which is related to various parts of nature and the evolving seasons.

Modern   Influence:
Irish legends and folklore keep on affecting current Irish culture, with large numbers of the old stories being retold in writing, craftsmanship, and film. These accounts are a significant piece of Ireland's social personality and are loved by individuals all over the planet.

All in all, Irish fables and folklore are a mother lode of stories and legends that have been passed down through the ages. They offer an interesting look into the convictions and customs of the old Celts and keep on enamoring crowds with their enchantment and secrets.

Traditional Irish music and dance

Customary Irish music and dance are essential pieces of Ireland's rich social legacy, mirroring the nation's set of experiences, values, and lifestyle. Established in old Celtic customs, these artistic expressions have advanced over hundreds of years and keep on being praised and appreciated by individuals all over the planet. Here is a thorough manual for conventional Irish music and dance:

Music:

Customary Irish music is described by its exuberant tunes, perplexing ornamentation, and cadenced examples. It is regularly played on instruments, for example, the fiddle, tin whistle, woodwind, uilleann pipes, and bodhrán (Irish drum). The music is played much of the time in a meeting, where performers accumulate in a bar or other casual environment to play together. Meetings are a significant piece of Irish melodic culture, giving a stage to performers to share and save customary tunes.

Dance:

Irish dance is known for its fast footwork, exact developments, and enthusiastic rhythms. It is often acted out in gatherings, with artists wearing elaborate outfits and shoes with hard soles that produce an unmistakable sound. The two most famous types of Irish dance are sean-nós (old style) and step-moving. Sean-nós is a performance dance that is described by its improvisational nature and close association with the music, while step-moving is a more organized structure that is in many cases acted out in gatherings.

Instruments:

The fiddle is maybe the most notorious instrument in customary Irish music, known for its sweet and vivacious sound. Different instruments usually utilized in Irish music incorporate the tin whistle, woodwind, uilleann pipes, and bodhrán. Each instrument has its own unique sound and job in the music, with the bodhrán giving a cadenced spine, the flute and whistle adding song, and the lines adding a frightful, ethereal quality.

Regional Variations:

Customary Irish music and dance change from one district to another, with every region having its own special style and collection. For instance, the music of Region Clare is known for its quick, driving rhythms, while the music of Donegal is described by its many-sided tunes. Likewise, various styles of dance are famous in various parts of Ireland, with certain districts leaning toward sean-nós and others inclining toward step-moving.

Influence and Revival:

Customary Irish music and dance have encountered a recovery in recent years, with numerous youngsters taking up these works of art and integrating them into contemporary music and dance styles. Associations, for example, Comhaltas Ceoltóirí Éireann play, had a vital impact in advancing and saving conventional Irish music and dance, sorting out contests, celebrations, and occasions to grandstand these fine arts.

Conventional Irish music and dance fundamentally affect music and dance styles all over the planet, impacting classes like nation, country, and people's music. Irish dance has likewise acquired fame through shows, for example, Riverdance and Master of the Dance, which have carried Irish dance to a worldwide crowd.

All in all, customary Irish music and dance are energetic and dynamic artistic expressions that proceed to flourish and develop. They are a significant piece of Ireland's social personality, praising the nation's set of experiences, legacy, and feeling of the local area.

Gaelic language and phrases

Gaelic, otherwise called Irish Gaelic or Gaeilge, is a Celtic language local to Ireland. It is perhaps the most established composed language in Europe, with a rich scholarly tradition dating back more than 1,500 years. Gaelic is a significant piece of Ireland's social personality, and endeavors are being made to save and advance the language. Here is a far-reaching manual for Gaelic language and expressions:

History and Origins:
Gaelic is an individual from the Goidelic part of the Celtic dialects, which likewise incorporates Scottish Gaelic and Manx. It is accepted to have developed from a typical Celtic language spoken in Ireland, something like quite a while ago. The earliest written accounts of Gaelic date back to the fifth century, with the record of ogham engravings on stone landmarks. The language prospered during the middle age time frame, delivering a rich group of writing, including legendary stories, verse, and strict texts.

"Phonetics and Grammar":
Gaelic is known for its mind-boggling phonetic framework, which remembers sounds not found in English. It has a rich arrangement of vowels and consonants, with a specific accentuation on the

utilization of suctioned and velarized consonants. The punctuation of Gaelic is likewise not quite the same as English, with a mind-boggling arrangement of action word formation, thing declension, and linguistic orientation. The language likewise has a particular word request, with the action word frequently showing up toward the start of the sentence.

Dia dhuit (DEE-uh gwitch) Hi (to one individual)
 Dia is Muire dhuit (DEE-uh iss MUR-uh gwitch) - Hi (answer)
Go raibh maith agat (guh fire up mah a-stomach).
Bless   your   heart.
Sláinte (SLAWN-cheh) Cheers (utilized while toasting)
Go raibh míle maith agat (guh fire up MEE-leh mah a-Stomach)   -   Thank   you   kindly
 Slán (SLAWN): Farewell

Literary   Tradition:
Gaelic has a rich scholarly tradition, with numerous exemplary works of writing written in the language. The earliest realized Gaelic writing incorporates

amazing stories like the Táin Bó Cúailnge (The Cows Strike of Cooley) and the Lebor Gabála Érenn (The Book of Intrusions). Gaelic verse is additionally exceptionally respected, with artists like Seamus Heaney and W.B. Yeats created works that have been converted into numerous dialects.

Revival Efforts:

As of late, there has been a recharged interest in Gaelic language and culture, prompting endeavors to restore and advance the language. The Irish government has executed strategies to build the utilization of Gaelic in schools, media, and government foundations. Associations like Conradh na Gaeilge (The Gaelic Association) play a critical role in advancing the language by coordinating occasions and exercises to bring issues to light and energize its utilization.

Modern Usage:

Today, Gaelic is spoken by a small but committed local area of speakers in Ireland and all over the planet. It is shown in schools and colleges, and there are Gaelic-language radio and TV programs.

While English is the predominant language in Ireland, Gaelic keeps on assuming a significant part in the country's social life, filling in as an image of public character and legacy.

All in all, Gaelic is a remarkable and old language with a rich history and social importance. Notwithstanding the difficulties it faces, Gaelic proceeds to flourish and develop, filling in as a demonstration of the strength and essentialness of Ireland's phonetic legacy.

Literary heritage: Yeats, Joyce, and more

Ireland has a rich scholarly legacy that has produced probably the most celebrated essayists in the English language. From writers to authors, dramatists to writers, Irish writing significantly affects the universe of letters. Among the numerous scholarly figures that have risen up out of Ireland, W.B. Yeats and James Joyce stand apart as two of the most persuasive and worshiped essayists. Here is a thorough manual for Ireland's scholarly legacy, zeroing in on Yeats, Joyce, and other prominent essayists:

W.B. Yeats (1865–1939): William Head Slave Yeats is broadly viewed as one of the best artists of the twentieth century. His verse is known for its melodious magnificence, magical subjects, and profound association with Irish old stories and folklore. Yeats was a vital figure in the Irish Scholarly Restoration, a development that tried to resuscitate and advance Irish culture and customs. He helped to establish the Convent Theater, Ireland's public theater, and was a main impetus behind the restoration of customary Irish folktales and legends. A portion of Yeats' most popular works incorporate "The Lake Isle of Innisfree," "The Subsequent Coming," and "Easter, 1916." He was granted the Nobel Prize in Writing in 1923.

James Joyce (1882–1941): James Joyce is most popular for his book "Ulysses," which is broadly viewed as one of the best works of innovative writing. The novel is a rethinking of Homer's legendary sonnet "The Odyssey," set in Dublin throughout a solitary day. Joyce's composing style is described by its trial utilization of language, continuous flow account strategy, and lavishly point-by-point portrayals of regular daily existence. His other remarkable works incorporate the brief tale assortment "Dubliners" and the book "A Picture of the Craftsman as a Young Fellow."

Notwithstanding his disputable and testing style, Joyce's work has affected current writing, motivating ages of journalists and researchers.

Other Eminent Writers: Seamus Heaney (1939–2013): Heaney was a writer, dramatist, and interpreter who won the Nobel Prize in Writing in 1995. His work frequently investigated subjects of Irish character, governmental issues, and history. Oscar Wilde (1854–1900): Wilde was a dramatist, writer, and writer known for his mind, humor, and social critique. His works incorporate "The Image of Dorian Dark" and "The Significance of Being Sincere."

Samuel Beckett (1906–1989): Beckett was a dramatist, writer, and artist who won the Nobel Prize in Writing in 1969. His most renowned work, "Hanging tight for Godot," is a fundamental work of innovative theater.

Literary Topics and Influence: Irish writing is known for its investigation of topics like personality, patriotism, religion, and the human condition. Journalists frequently draw on Irish legends, folklore, and history to investigate these subjects.

Crafted by Irish journalists, it has impacted world writing, with numerous authors referring to Yeats, Joyce, and others as having significant impacts. Their work keeps on being considered, examined, and celebrated by researchers and perusers all over the planet.

All in all, Ireland's scholarly legacy is a demonstration of the country's rich social and creative heritage. Authors like Yeats, Joyce, and others have left a permanent imprint on the universe of writing, moving ages of essayists and perusers with their significant bits of knowledge, wonderful excellence, and innovative narrating.

Chapter 7: Top Places Off the Beaten Path

The Aran Islands

The Aran Islands, situated off the west shoreline of Ireland, are a gathering of three islands—Inishmore (Árainn), Inishmaan (Inis Meáin), and Inisheer (Inis Oírr)—known for their tough excellence, rich social legacy, and conventional lifestyle. These islands offer guests a brief look into a lifestyle that has remained to a great extent unaltered for a really long time, making them a well-known location for those trying to encounter the credible excellence of Ireland's west coast. Here is a far-reaching manual for investigating the Aran Islands:

History   and   Heritage: The Aran Islands have a rich history dating back millennia, with proof of human settlement dating all the way back to ancient times. The islands are home to various old remnants, including stone strongholds, temples, and religious locales, which offer an interesting look into Ireland's past. The islands are likewise known for major areas of strength in their legacy, with a rich practice of music, dance, and narrating. Guests to the islands can immerse themselves in this lively culture by going to customary music meetings and widespread developments.

Natural   Beauty:

The Aran Islands are eminent for their staggering normal magnificence, with tough shorelines, sensational bluffs, and clearing vistas. The islands are a heaven for nature sweethearts, with an assortment of vegetation to find. Perhaps one of the most famous landmarks on the islands is Dun Aonghasa, an ancient stone post roosted on the edge of a 100-meter precipice. The stronghold offers dazzling perspectives on the encompassing scene and is a must-visit objective for guests to the islands.

Activities   and   Attractions:

The Aran Islands offer a scope of exercises for guests to appreciate, from climbing and cycling to kayaking and fishing. The islands are likewise a well-known objective for birdwatching, with various seabirds settling on the precipices. Notwithstanding open-air exercises, the Aran Islands are home to various social attractions, including historical centers, displays, and art shops, where guests can find out about the islands' rich history and legacy.

Local Life and Traditions: One of the features of a visit to the Aran Islands is encountering the customary lifestyle that has been protected on the islands. The islands are home to an affectionate local area of inhabitants who keep on rehearsing conventional specialties and exchanges.

Guests to the islands can submerge themselves in this remarkable lifestyle by visiting nearby craftsmen and skilled workers, going to customary music meetings, and testing neighborhood cooking.

Practical Information: The Aran Islands are open by ship from the central area, with ordinary administrations leaving from the towns of Doolin and Rossaveal. The ships offer staggering perspectives on the islands and the encompassing shore. Convenience on the islands goes from guesthouses and overnight boarding houses to self-providing food bungalows and campgrounds. It's prudent to book convenience ahead of time, particularly during the peak mid-year months.

All in all, the Aran Islands offer an extraordinary and true look into Ireland's history over a significant time span. With their dazzling regular magnificence, rich social legacy, and customary lifestyle, these islands are a must-visit objective for anybody trying to encounter the genuine quintessence of Ireland's west coast.

Connemara National Park

Connemara Public Park, situated in Region Galway in the west of Ireland, is a shocking spread of wilderness known for its tough excellence, unblemished scenes, and rich biodiversity. Covering an area of roughly 2,000 hectares, the recreation area is home to different natural surroundings, including mountains, lowlands, heaths, and forests, making it a safe house for untamed life and a heaven for outside fans. Here is a far-reaching manual for investigating Connemara Public Park:

History and Heritage:
Connemara Public Park was laid out in 1980 and is one of six public parks in Ireland. The recreation area is named after the Connemara district, which is known for its wild and untamed magnificence. The recreation area is home to various archeological locales, including massive burial chambers, old settlements, and middle-age ruins, which offer an intriguing look into Ireland's old past.

Natural Beauty:
The scene of Connemara Public Park is portrayed by its rough mountains, far-reaching lowlands, and serene lakes. One of the recreation area's most notorious highlights is the Twelve Bens mountain range, which overwhelms the horizon and offers amazing perspectives on the encompassing open country.
The recreation area is likewise home to different

plant and creature species, including intriguing orchids, wild horses, and red deer. Birdwatchers will likewise get a kick out of the recreation area's different birdlife, including scavengers, kestrels, and peregrine hawks.

Activities and Attractions: Connemara Public Park offers a scope of exercises for guests to appreciate, including climbing, cycling, and horseback riding. There are various all-around checked trails all through the recreation area, going from simple strolls to more difficult climbs. One of the most well-known trails is the Precious Stone Slope Circle, a 7-kilometer circle trail that takes explorers to the culmination of Jewel Slope, the most noteworthy point in the recreation area. From the culmination, climbers can appreciate all encompassing perspectives on the encompassing open country.

The recreation area is likewise home to a guest community, which highlights intuitive displays of the recreation area's regular and social history. The middle additionally offers directed strolls and talks, furnishing guests with an understanding of the recreation area's interesting environment.

Local Life and Traditions:
The Connemara district is known for areas of strength in its legacy, with a rich practice of music, dance, and narrating. Guests to the recreation area can immerse themselves in this lively culture by going to customary music meetings and widespread developments. The recreation area is likewise home to various little towns and networks, where guests can encounter the conventional lifestyle that has been safeguarded in this remote corner of Ireland.

Practical Information:
Connemara Public Park is open all year, and confirmation is free. The recreation area is found around 20 kilometers west of the town of Clifden, which is the biggest town in the Connemara locale. Convenience in the space goes from guesthouses and overnight boarding houses to self-catering bungalows and campgrounds. It's fitting to book convenience ahead of time, particularly during the pinnacle of the late spring months.

All in all, Connemara Public Park is a mother lode of normal magnificence and social legacy, offering guests an extraordinary chance to investigate Ireland's wild and untamed west. Whether you're climbing through the mountains, birdwatching in the lowlands, or submerging yourself in the neighborhood culture, Connemara Public Park makes certain to leave you with recollections that will endure forever.

The Dingle Peninsula

The Dingle Promontory, situated in Area Kerry in the southwest of Ireland, is eminent for its shocking waterfront landscape, rich social legacy, and dynamic Gaelic culture. Extending out into the Atlantic Sea, the landmass is home to a portion of Ireland's most stunning scenery, from rough precipices and sandy seashores to moving slopes and beautiful towns. Here is an exhaustive manual for investigating the Dingle Promontory:

History and Heritage: The Dingle Promontory is saturated with history, with proof of human settlement dating back more than 6,000 years. The promontory is home to various old locales, including colony of bee cabins, ring posts, and Ogham stones, which offer a brief look into Ireland's old past. The landmass is likewise known for its rich Christian legacy, with various early Christian destinations, including places of worship and religious communities, dispersed all through the area.

Natural   Beauty:
The Dingle Promontory is famous for its dazzling regular excellence, with rough precipices, unblemished seashores, and moving slopes. Perhaps the most famous milestone on the landmass is Slea Head, the westernmost point in Ireland, which offers all-encompassing perspectives on the Atlantic Sea and the Blasket Islands. The landmass is likewise home to different plant and creature species, including intriguing orchids, seals, and dolphins. Birdwatchers will likewise thoroughly enjoy the landmass's assorted birdlife, including puffins, gannets, and shearwaters.

Activities and Attractions:
The Single Landmass offers a scope of exercises for guests to appreciate, including climbing, cycling, and water sports. There are various very well-checked trails all through the landmass, going from simple strolls to more difficult climbs. The landmass is likewise home to various enchanting towns and villages, including Dingle Town, which is well known for its conventional music and dynamic nightlife. Guests can investigate the town's limited roads, visit its numerous bars and cafés, and test neighborhood cooking.

Cultural Experiences:
The Single Landmass is home to a lively Gaelic culture, with the Irish language actually spoken in many pieces of the promontory. Guests to the area can submerge themselves in this rich social legacy by going to conventional music meetings, narrating occasions, and Gaelic language classes. The promontory is additionally known for its specialties and artworks, with numerous

neighborhood craftsmen creating conventional Irish merchandise like stoneware, materials, and gems. Guests can visit nearby art shops and displays to buy these one-of-a kind and genuine things.

Practical   Information:

The Single Landmass is available via vehicle or transport from the town of Tralee, which is the biggest town in Area Kerry. The landmass is roughly 50 kilometers in length and can be investigated in a day, although numerous guests decide to endure a few days investigating its numerous   attractions.

Convenience in the space goes from guesthouses and overnight boarding houses to self-providing food houses and campgrounds. It's prudent to book convenience ahead of time, particularly during the pinnacle of the late spring months.

All in all, the Dingle Promontory is a gold mine of normal excellence, history, and culture, offering guests a novel chance to encounter the best of Ireland's west coast. Whether you're investigating old remains, climbing along rough precipices, or submerging yourself in the nearby culture, the

Dingle Promontory makes certain to leave you with recollections that will endure forever.

The Burren

While arranging an excursion to Ireland, finding the right convenience is critical to an agreeable and charming stay. Ireland offers an extensive variety of convenience choices to suit each financial plan and inclination, from lavish inns to enchanting informal lodging, financially cordial inns, and comfortable guesthouses. Here is an outline of the convenience choices accessible in Ireland:

Hotels:
Ireland brags a wide range of inns, from extravagant five-star foundations to more reasonable three-star choices. Lodgings in Ireland are known for their warm cordiality, agreeable facilities, and magnificent conveniences. Numerous lodgings in Ireland are situated in notable structures, offering visitors an opportunity to encounter the country's rich legacy. A few

lodgings likewise include nearby eateries, spas, and recreation offices.

Bed and Morning Meals (B&Bs): B&Bs are a well-known convenience decision in Ireland, offering visitors an opportunity to remain in a family-run home and experience the warm friendliness of the Irish public. B&Bs in Ireland are known for their agreeable facilities, scrumptious home-prepared morning meals, and customized administration.

B&Bs are ordinarily more reasonable than inns and offer a more close and true Irish experience. Numerous B&Bs are situated in grand rustic areas, offering visitors an opportunity to encounter Ireland's staggering open country.

Hostels:

Lodgings are a financial plan accommodating convenience choices in Ireland, especially among youthful voyagers and hikers. Lodgings in Ireland offer dorm-style facilities as well as confidential rooms and are an extraordinary method for meeting individual explorers.

Lodgings in Ireland are known for their loose and

agreeable environment, as well as their common regions where visitors can mingle and trade travel tips. Numerous lodgings additionally offer conveniences like free Wi-Fi, clothing offices, and shared kitchens.

Guesthouses:

Guesthouses in Ireland offer a more plain and cozy convenience experience, like B&Bs, but frequently with fewer rooms. Guesthouses are regularly family-run and offer a warm greeting to visitors. Guesthouses in Ireland are known for their agreeable facilities, delightful morning meals, and customized administration. Numerous guesthouses are situated in noteworthy structures, offering visitors an opportunity to encounter Ireland's rich history and culture.

Practical   Tips:

While booking convenience in Ireland, it's fitting to book ahead of time, particularly during the pinnacle vacationer season (June to August) and for famous locations like Dublin, Galway, and Killarney. It's likewise really smart to check the area of your convenience according to the attractions you intend to visit. Numerous attractions in Ireland are situated in country regions, so approaching a vehicle might be   fundamental. At long last, make certain to pursue audits of convenience choices prior to booking to guarantee that they measure up to your assumptions. Sites, for example, TripAdvisor and Booking.com, are helpful assets for tracking down convenience and perusing audits from different explorers.

All in all, Ireland offers an extensive variety of convenience choices to suit each financial plan and inclination, from rich lodgings to enchanting B&Bs, well-disposed lodgings, and comfortable guesthouses. Whether you're searching for a lavish retreat or a financially accommodating spot to rest your head, Ireland has something for everybody.

Chapter 8: Accommodations

Overview of accommodation options: hotels, B&Bs, hostels, and guesthouses

While arranging an outing to Ireland, finding the right convenience is vital to an agreeable and charming stay. Ireland offers an extensive variety of convenience choices to suit each financial plan and inclination, from lavish lodgings to beguiling overnight boarding houses, financially well-disposed inns, and comfortable guesthouses. Here is an outline of the convenience choices accessible in Ireland:

Hotels:

Ireland boasts a wide range of lodgings, from rich five-star foundations to more reasonable three-star choices. Lodgings in Ireland are known for their warm neighborliness, agreeable facilities, and great conveniences.

Numerous lodgings in Ireland are situated in noteworthy structures, offering visitors an opportunity to encounter the country's rich legacy. A few lodgings likewise include nearby cafés, spas, and relaxation offices.

Bed and Morning Meals (B&Bs): B&Bs are a famous convenience decision in Ireland, offering visitors an opportunity to remain in a family-run home and experience the warm cordiality of the Irish public. B&Bs in Ireland are known for their agreeable facilities, heavenly home-prepared morning meals, and customized administration.

B&Bs are normally more reasonable than lodgings and offer a more cozy and legitimate Irish experience. Numerous B&Bs are situated in picturesque rustic areas, offering visitors an opportunity to encounter Ireland's shockingly open country.

Hostels:

Lodgings are a well-disposed convenience choice in Ireland, especially among youthful explorers and hikers. Lodgings in Ireland offer dorm-style facilities as well as confidential rooms and are an extraordinary method for meeting individual explorers.

Lodgings in Ireland are known for their loose and amicable air, as well as their common regions where visitors can mingle and trade travel tips. Numerous lodgings likewise offer conveniences like free Wi-Fi, clothing offices, and shared kitchens.

Guesthouses:

Guesthouses in Ireland offer a more simple and personal convenience experience, like B&Bs, but frequently with fewer rooms. Guesthouses are ordinarily family-run and offer a warm greeting to visitors.

Guesthouses in Ireland are known for their agreeable facilities, scrumptious morning meals, and customized administration. Numerous guesthouses are situated in notable structures, offering visitors an opportunity to encounter Ireland's rich history and culture.

Practical   Tips:

While booking convenience in Ireland, it's prudent to book ahead of time, particularly during the pinnacle traveler season (June to August) and for famous destinations like Dublin, Galway, and Killarney.

It's likewise really smart to check the area of your convenience corresponding to the attractions you intend to visit. Numerous attractions in Ireland are situated in provincial regions, so approaching a vehicle might be essential. At long last, make certain to peruse surveys of convenience choices prior to booking to guarantee that they measure up to your assumptions. Sites, for example, TripAdvisor and Booking.com, are valuable assets for tracking down convenience and pursuing audits from different explorers.

All in all, Ireland offers an extensive variety of convenience choices to suit each financial plan and inclination, from lavish lodgings to enchanting

B&Bs, spending-plan cordial lodgings, and comfortable guesthouses. Whether you're searching for a lavish retreat or a financially accommodating spot to rest your head, Ireland has something for everybody.

Recommended hotels in major cities and tourist areas

While going to Ireland, picking the right lodging can enormously upgrade your experience. Whether you're searching for extravagance facilities, beguiling shop inns, or spending plan cordial choices, Ireland has a large number of lodgings to suit each explorer's requirements. Here are a few suggested lodgings in significant urban communities and travel regions:

The Shelbourne, Autograph Collection: Situated in the core of Dublin, this memorable lodging offers lavish facilities and perfect assistance. It's near top attractions like Trinity School and Grafton Road.

The Westbury Hotel: Arranged close to Dublin's renowned shopping locale, this five-star inn offers rich rooms and suites, along with a range of eating choices and a wellness place.

The Morrison Dublin, Curio Collection by Hilton: This jazzy lodging disregards the Waterway Liffey and offers contemporary rooms, a stylish bar, and simple access to Dublin's nightlife and social attractions.

Galway:

The G Hotel & Spa: Known for its special plan and lavish conveniences, this five-star inn offers staggering perspectives on Lough Atalia and is a short stroll from Eyre Square and Galway's clamoring downtown area.

The Connacht Hotel: a family-accommodating inn with roomy rooms, recreation offices, and a variety of dining choices. It's found right outside the Galway downtown area, making it a helpful base for investigating the region.

The House Hotel: Arranged in the core of Galway's Latin Quarter, this store offers a la carte facilities and simple access to the city's shops, bars, and eateries.

Killarney:

The Europe Lodging and Resort: Set on the shores of Lough Leane, this lavish inn offers stunning perspectives on the lake and mountains. It highlights rich rooms, a spa, and award-winning feasting choices.

The Killarney Park Hotel: Situated at the focal point of Killarney, this five-star inn offers extravagant facilities, a spa, and top-notch food choices. It's within strolling distance of Killarney Public Park and its attractions.

The Brehon: A four-star lodging known for its warm cordiality and contemporary plan. It's situated close to the INEC Killarney and a short stroll from Killarney town center.

Cork:

The River Lee: Settled on the banks of the

Waterway Lee, this lavish inn offers trendy rooms, a spa, and a variety of dining choices. It's within strolling distance of the Stopper downtown area and its attractions.

The Imperial Hotel is a notable inn situated in the core of the Plug downtown area, offering rich facilities and a variety of eating choices. It's near Stopper's shops, eateries, and social attractions.

The Metropole Hotel: Arranged in the Stopper downtown area, this four-star inn offers agreeable facilities, a relaxation place, and simple access to Plug's attractions and nightlife.

These are only a couple of the numerous brilliant inns Ireland brings to the table. Whether you're searching for extravagance facilities, enchanting shop lodgings, or spending plan cordial choices, you're certain to track down the ideal spot to remain in Ireland.

Tips for booking accommodations and finding the right fit for your trip

Booking facilities for your excursion to Ireland can be an overwhelming undertaking, with such countless choices accessible. In any case, with just enough examination and arranging, you can track down the ideal spot to remain that suits your requirements and financial plan. Here are a few methods for booking facilities and tracking down an ideal choice for your outing:

Start Early: It's prudent to begin searching for convenience as soon as could really be expected, particularly in the event that you're going during the peak vacationer season (June to August) or to famous locations. This will give you more choices and better rates.

Set a Budget: Before you begin searching for convenience, set a financial plan for your outing. This will assist you with reducing your choices and abstaining from overspending.

Consider Location: While picking convenience, consider its area according to the attractions you intend to visit. In the event that you're wanting to investigate a specific region, it very well might merit paying a smidgen more to remain nearer to your ideal area.

Read Reviews: Prior to booking convenience, read audits from different explorers on sites like TripAdvisor or Booking.com. This will provide you with a sense of the nature of the convenience and the encounters of different visitors.

Check Amenities: Search for conveniences that offer the conveniences you want for an agreeable stay, for example, free Wi-Fi, breakfast included, or a pool. Try to check in the event that there are any extra charges for these conveniences.

Consider the Sort of Accommodation: Think about the kind of convenience that suits your necessities and inclinations. Whether you favor an inn, quaint little inn, or guesthouse, there are a lot of choices accessible in Ireland.

Look for arrangements and discounts: Watch out for arrangements and limits on convenience sites or through travel services. You might have the option to find exceptional offers or bundles that can assist you with setting aside cash.

Book Straightforwardly with the Hotel: At times, booking straightforwardly with the lodging can set aside your cash compared with booking through an outsider site. Additionally, it gives you greater adaptability with regards to changes or abrogations.

Consider Elective Convenience Options: notwithstanding customary lodgings, consider elective convenience choices like Airbnb, get-away rentals, or ranch stays. These can offer a remarkable and critical experience while frequently being more reasonable than lodgings.

Be Adaptable with Your Dates: Assuming conceivable, be adaptable with your movement dates. Convenience costs can fluctuate fundamentally contingent upon the season, so changing your dates marginally could bring about huge investment funds.

By following these tips, you can track down the ideal convenience for your outing to Ireland that addresses your issues and financial plan, guaranteeing an agreeable and charming stay.

Chapter 9: Health Tips and Safety Information

Medical services and facilities in Ireland

While venturing out to Ireland, it's critical to know about the clinical benefits and offices accessible on the off chance that you want clinical help during your excursion. Ireland has an exclusive requirement of medical services, with both public and confidential medical care choices accessible. Here is a complete manual for clinical benefits and offices in Ireland:

Public Medical services System: - Ireland has a public medical services framework, known as the Wellbeing Administration Chief (HSE), which offers clinical types of assistance to inhabitants and guests. The framework is supported through broad tax collection and gives a scope of administrations, including clinic care, essential consideration, and crisis administrations.

- Guests from EU/EEA nations are qualified for get crisis clinical treatment under the European Medical coverage Card (EHIC) conspire. It's prudent to convey a legitimate EHIC card with you while heading out to Ireland.

- Non-EU/EEA guests are not qualified with the expectation of complementary medical services and are encouraged to have travel protection that covers clinical costs.

Private   Healthcare:

- Confidential medical care in Ireland is likewise accessible, with numerous confidential medical clinics and centers offering a scope of administrations. Confidential medical services can be more costly than public medical care however may offer more limited holding up times and more conveniences.

- Numerous confidential clinics and facilities in Ireland take care of the two occupants and guests and acknowledge worldwide health care coverage plans. It's fitting to check with your protection supplier prior to looking for treatment.

Hospitals and Clinics:

- Ireland has various medical clinics and centers situated all through the country, both public and private. Significant urban communities like Dublin, Stopper, and Galway have a few emergency clinics offering a scope of clinical benefits.

- In the event of a crisis, dial 999 or 112 to arrive at the crisis administrations. The administrator will dispatch a rescue vehicle to take you to the closest medical clinic.

Pharmacies:

- Drug stores in Ireland (known as scientific experts) are generally accessible and can be tracked down in many towns and urban communities. Drug stores stock a scope of non-prescription meds as well as physician endorsed meds.

- In the event that you want a physician recommended medicine, you should see a specialist or visit a facility to get medicine.

Health Dangers and Precautions:

- Ireland is a generally protected objective as far as wellbeing chances. Be that as it may, it's prudent to play it safe against normal ailments like colds, influenza, and stomach bugs.

It's additionally prescribed to have modern immunizations prior to venturing out to Ireland, especially for sicknesses like measles, mumps, and rubella (MMR) and flu.

Travel   Insurance:
It is emphatically prescribed that travel protection cover clinical costs, including crisis clinical treatment, clinic stays, and bringing home. This can provide true serenity and monetary security in the event of surprising clinical issues.

All in all, Ireland has an elevated expectation of medical services, with both public and confidential choices accessible. By monitoring the clinical benefits and offices in Ireland, you can guarantee that you will receive the consideration you want in the event of health-related crises during your outing.

Health insurance coverage and recommendations

While arranging an outing to Ireland, it's critical to consider your health care coverage inclusion to guarantee you're ready for any health-related crises that might emerge during your movements. Here is an extensive manual for health care coverage inclusion and proposals for voyagers to Ireland:

European Health Care Coverage Card (EHIC):

In the event that you're a resident of an EU/EEA nation or Switzerland, it's fitting to convey a substantial European Health Care Coverage Card (EHIC) while heading out to Ireland. The EHIC qualifies you to get essential clinical treatment at diminished cost or, at times, for nothing in Ireland.

The EHIC covers therapy that turns out to be medicinally essential during your visit, and it likewise covers previous ailments and routine maternity care, for however long you're not going for the express reason for acquiring clinical treatment.

Non-EU/EEA Travelers:

Non-EU/EEA explorers are not qualified with the expectation of complementary medical care in Ireland and are encouraged to have travel protection that covers clinical costs. Travel protection ought to incorporate inclusion for crisis clinical therapy, emergency clinic stays, and bringing home in the event of a health-related crisis.

Private Wellbeing Insurance:

In the event that you have private health care coverage in your nation of origin, check with your insurance supplier to see whether your contract covers clinical costs in Ireland. Some confidential health care coverage plans offer worldwide inclusion or can be stretched out to cover travel abroad.

Travel Insurance:

It's unequivocally prescribed for all voyagers to Ireland to have travel protection that incorporates clinical service. Travel protection can provide monetary security in the event of startling clinical issues, like sickness, injury, or clinical departure.

While buying travel insurance, try to peruse the contract cautiously to comprehend what is covered, including clinical costs, crisis clearing, trip retraction, and other misfortune or postponement.

Coverage   Recommendations:

Guarantee that your movement protection gives satisfactory inclusion to clinical costs, including medical clinic stays, medical procedures, and crisis clinical   transportation.

Check in the event that your movement protection covers prior ailments as well as exercises, for example, sports or sporting exercises that you intend to partake in during your excursion. - Confirm that your movement protection incorporates inclusion for trip undoing or interference, as well as lost or taken effects, to give extensive security during your movements.

Emergency   Assistance:

In the event of a health-related crisis, dial 999 or 112 to reach the crisis administrations in Ireland. The administrator will dispatch an emergency vehicle to take you to the closest clinic. - Convey a duplicate of your movement insurance contract and contact data for your protection supplier with you consistently, in the event that you want to look for clinical treatment or record a case.

All in all, having satisfactory health care coverage inclusion is fundamental while heading out to Ireland to guarantee you approach clinical consideration if there should be an occurrence of crises. Whether you have an EHIC, confidential health care coverage, or travel protection, make a point to grasp your inclusion and convey the vital documentation with you during your excursion.

Tips for staying healthy while traveling

Remaining sound while heading out is fundamental to partaking in your excursion to Ireland. Whether you're investigating the clamoring roads of Dublin or climbing through the picturesque open country, it's vital to deal with your wellbeing to guarantee a protected and pleasant experience. Here are a few methods for remaining sound while voyaging:

Stay   Hydrated:

Drink a lot of water over the course of the day, particularly in the event that you're participating in proactive tasks or investing energy outside. Lack of hydration can prompt exhaustion, cerebral pains, and other medical problems.

Eat   a   Decent   Diet:

Attempt to keep a decent eating regimen while traveling, consolidating a lot of natural products, vegetables, and whole grains into your dinners. Stay away from exorbitant utilization of unfortunate food sources and liquor.

Practice   Great   Hygiene:

Clean up much of the time with a cleanser and water, particularly prior to eating or subsequent to utilizing the bathroom. Use hand sanitizer when cleanser   and   water   are   not   available.
Convey a movement-measured hand sanitizer with you for added comfort.

Get a lot of rest:

Guarantee you get a satisfactory measure of rest every night to assist your body with recuperating from the day's exercises and remaining solid.

On the off chance that you're encountering plane slack, attempt to conform to the nearby time region as fast as conceivable by getting open to regular light during the day and staying away from rests.

Stay Active:

Integrate actual work into your day-to-day everyday practice, like strolling, climbing, or cycling. This can assist you with remaining calm and stimulated during your excursion.

Numerous urban communities and towns in Ireland offer strolling visits or bicycle rentals, which are extraordinary ways of investigating the region while remaining dynamic.

Protect Yourself from the Sun:

Ireland's weather conditions can be capricious; however, even on overcast days, it's critical to safeguard your skin from the sun's destructive UV beams. Wear sunscreen with a high SPF and reapply consistently, particularly in the event that you're investing energy outside. Think about wearing a cap and shades for added security.

Be Arranged for Climate Changes: Ireland's weather conditions can change rapidly, so it's vital to be ready for a wide range of climates. Pack layers that you can without much of a stretch add or eliminate on a case-by-case basis. Convey a little umbrella or overcoat with you in the event of a downpour.

Stay informed about wellbeing risks: Prior to heading out to Ireland, get to know if any wellbeing takes a chance with the area you'll visit. This can incorporate normal ailments, like colds or influenza, as well as any nearby wellbeing warnings. Consider getting travel protection that covers clinical costs in the event that you really want to look for clinical treatment while abroad.

By following these tips, you can help guarantee a solid and pleasant outing to Ireland. Make sure to pay attention to your body, enjoy reprieves when required, and look for clinical consideration if you begin feeling unwell.

Chapter 10: Practical Tips and Useful Information

Public transportation information and tips

Public transportation in Ireland is a helpful and proficient method for investigating the nation, particularly on the off chance that you're visiting urban communities like Dublin, Stopper, Galway, or Limerick. Here is a far-reaching manual for public transportation in Ireland, including data and ways to utilize transports, trains, and cable cars:

Buses:

Transport Éireann works on an exhaustive transport network that interfaces urban communities, towns, and provincial regions across Ireland. The transports are agreeable and furnished with present-day conveniences, making them a helpful choice for voyagers.

In urban communities like Dublin, Stopper, Galway, and Limerick, there are additional neighborhood transport benefits that provide transportation inside the city and its rural areas. These administrations are in many cases worked by various organizations, so checking timetables and courses prior to traveling is prudent.

To involve transport in Ireland, you can buy tickets straightforwardly from the transport driver or at transport stations. It's likewise conceivable to purchase tickets ahead of time on the web or through portable applications for specific courses.

Trains:

Irish Rail (Iarnród Éireann) operates the public rail network in Ireland, offering services between significant urban areas and towns. The trains are agreeable and give beautiful perspectives on the open country.

The DART (Dublin Region Fast Travel) is a rural rail administration that works in the Dublin region, providing speedy and helpful transportation between the downtown area and rural areas along the coast.

To involve trains in Ireland, you can buy tickets at train stations, on the web, or through versatile applications. It's fitting to book tickets ahead of time for significant distance ventures, particularly during peak travel times.

Trams:

The Luas is a light rail cable car framework that works in Dublin, providing transportation between the downtown area and rural areas. The Luas comprises two lines: the Green Line and the Red Line, which associate various pieces of the city.

To utilize the Luas, you can buy tickets at Luas stations or on board the cable cars. There are also ticket machines at stations where you can purchase tickets using money or a card.

Tips for Utilizing Public Transportation:

Plan Your Excursion: Prior to traveling, actually look at timetables and courses for transports, trains, and cable cars to guarantee you arrive at your destination on time.

Buy Tickets Ahead of Time: For significant distance ventures or during top travel times, it's prudent to book tickets ahead of time to get your seat.

Use Applications for Continuous Data: Numerous public transportation administrations in Ireland have portable applications that give constant data on timetables, courses, and postponements.

Be Aware of Pinnacle Travel Times: Public transportation can be more occupied during peak travel times, so plan as needed and permit additional time for your excursion.

Regard Different Travelers: Be kind to different travelers and adhere to the guidelines and guidelines of the transportation administration.

Remain Safe: Keep your assets secure and know about your environmental factors, particularly in packed regions.

Generally speaking, public transportation in Ireland is a helpful and dependable method for investigating the country. By really getting to know the different transportation choices and following these tips, you can partake in a smooth and charming excursion across Ireland.

Driving in Ireland: rules of the road and car rental tips

Driving in Ireland can be a great method for investigating the country's grand scenes and memorable destinations. Be that as it may, it's critical to get to know the standards of the street and vehicle rental tips to guarantee a protected and pleasant excursion. Here is an exhaustive manual for driving in Ireland:

Rules of the Road:
In Ireland, vehicles drive on the left half of the street, and the guiding wheel is on the right half of the vehicle.

As far as possible, in Ireland, it is as follows: 50 km/h in developed regions, 80 km/h on local streets, and 100 km/h on public streets. Speed limits are completely implemented, and speeding can bring about fines or punishments.

Safety belts are obligatory for all travelers in the vehicle, and youngsters under 12 years of age should exercise proper self-control.

It is against the law to utilize a cell phone while

driving, except if you have a hands-free framework. Punishments for utilizing a cell phone while driving can include fines, and punishment focuses on your permit.

Road   Conditions:

Street conditions in Ireland are, for the most part, great, with roads and streets very much kept up. In any case, country streets can be limited and twisting, so it means a lot to drive with alertness, particularly   in   new   regions.

Know about nearby street signs and markings, as they might differ from those in your nation of origin. Focus on street signs demonstrating speed limits, street conditions, and possible perils.

Driving   Etiquette:

Irish drivers are by and large obliging and honest, yet it's essential to know about neighborhood driving traditions. Be ready for traffic circles, which are normal in Ireland, and respect traffic currently in the   traffic   circle.

While driving on slender streets, be ready to head over to permit approaching cars to pass. Utilize your pointers to flag your goal to pull over.

Know about animals on rustic streets, particularly in horticultural regions. Drive gradually, and be ready to stop if it is fundamental.

Car   Rental   Tips:

To lease a vehicle in Ireland, you should be no less than 21 years of age (age might fluctuate by rental organization) and have a substantial driver's permit from your nation of origin. A few rental organizations may likewise require a Worldwide Driving   License   (IDP).

While leasing a vehicle, make certain to check the protection inclusions presented by the rental organization. Think about buying extra protection inclusion, for example, an impact harm waiver (CDW) or abundance protection, to safeguard yourself against surprising costs if there should arise   an   occurrence   of   a   mishap.

Know about the fuel strategy of the rental organization. A few organizations expect you to return the vehicle with a full tank of fuel, while others might offer the choice to prepay for fuel and return   the   vehicle   vacant.

Prior to driving off, investigate the vehicle for any current harm and make note of it on the tenant contract. Take photographs of any harm to keep away from debates while returning the vehicle. Get to know the vehicle's controls, including the lights, windshield wipers, and danger lights. Know that speed cutoff points and distances in Ireland are estimated in kilometers.

By observing these guidelines for the street and vehicle rental tips, you can partake in a protected and noteworthy driving experience in Ireland.

Internet and communication options for travelers

Remaining associated while going to Ireland is significant for keeping in contact with friends and family, getting access to data, and exploring your strategy for getting around. Here is a complete manual for web and correspondence choices for explorers in Ireland:

Mobile Networks:

Ireland has a few versatile organization administrators, including Vodafone, Three, Eir, and Tesco Portable, offering a range of paid-ahead and postpaid plans.

Buying a nearby SIM card can be a practical method for remaining connected during your excursion. You can purchase a SIM card at cell phone shops, general stores, or at the air terminal.

Mobile Data:

Versatile information is broadly accessible in Ireland, with 4G inclusion in most metropolitan regions and 3G inclusion in country regions. A few administrators likewise offer 5G inclusion in significant urban communities.

Information plans shift in cost and information remittance, so looking at plans prior to purchasing is prudent. You can top up your information remittance, depending on the situation, through your portable administrator's site or application.

Wi-Fi:

Wi-Fi is broadly accessible in lodgings, bistros, cafés, and vacation spots all through Ireland.

Numerous facilities offer free Wi-Fi to visitors; however, some might charge an expense or cutoff utilization.

It's prudent to utilize a virtual confidential organization (VPN) while interfacing with public Wi-Fi organizations to safeguard your own data and information.

Internet   Cafes:

Web bistros are more uncommon in Ireland than they used to be; however, you can in any case track them down in significant urban communities and traveler regions. They normally offer rapid web access for a charge.

Roaming:

In the event that you're going from an EU/EEA country, you can bring your cell phone in Ireland at no extra expense, on account of the EU's "Meander Like at Home" approach. Check with your versatile administrator to ensure your arrangement incorporates meandering in Ireland.

In the event that you're going from a non-EU or EA country, check with your versatile administrator about wandering charges and information plans for global travel.

Communication Apps:

Correspondence applications like WhatsApp, Skype, and Viber are famous and can be utilized to settle on decisions, send messages, and video talk over the web. These applications can be a practical method for keeping in contact with loved ones back home.

Try to download and set up these applications before you travel, and guarantee you have a steady web association with them.

Emergency Services:

In the event of a crisis, dial 999 or 112 to reach the crisis administration in Ireland. The administrator will interface you with the police, emergency vehicle, or fire administrations, depending on the situation.

It's prudent to have a rundown of crisis contacts, including nearby contacts and your international safe haven or department, saved in your telephone if there should be an occurrence of a crisis.

By exploiting these web and correspondence choices, you can remain associated and informed during your movements in Ireland.

Electricity and plug adapters

While venturing out to Ireland, it's vital to know about the country's power guidelines and the sort of attachment connector you'll have to utilize. Here is a far-reaching manual for power and plug connectors in Ireland:

Voltage and Frequency:
In Ireland, the standard voltage is 230 volts, and the recurrence is 50 Hz. This is unique in relation to the US and a few different nations, where the standard voltage is 120 volts and the recurrence is 60 Hz.

Prior to connecting any electronic gadgets, ensure they are viable with the Irish voltage and recurrence. Most present-day electronic gadgets, like workstations and cell phones, are double-voltage and can be utilized in Ireland without a voltage converter.

Plug   Adapters:

Ireland utilizes a Sort G plug, which has three rectangular prongs in a three-sided design. This is a similar type utilized in the Unified Realm and a few different nations.

On the off chance that your gadgets have an alternate kind of fitting, you will require an attachment connector to involve them in Ireland. Plug connectors are generally accessible at hardware stores, travel stores, and online retailers.

Voltage   Converters:

On the off chance that your electronic gadgets are not double-voltage, you will require a voltage converter to involve them in Ireland. A voltage converter changes the 230V voltage completely to the lower voltage expected by your gadgets.

It's critical to pick a voltage converter that is reasonable for your gadget's power requirements. Utilizing an inaccurate voltage converter can harm your gadgets.

Power   Outlets:

Electrical plugs in Ireland are intended to acknowledge Type G plugs. They are normally rectangular in shape, with three openings organized in a triangle design.

A few more seasoned structures in Ireland might have electrical plugs that are not grounded. In the event that you experience an ungrounded outlet, it's prudent to utilize a flood defender to safeguard your gadgets.

Travel   Connectors   versus   Converters:

It's critical to recognize plug connectors and voltage converters. A fitting connector just permits you to plug your gadgets into an alternate kind of power source, while a voltage converter really changes the voltage over completely to match the necessities of your gadgets.

In the event that your gadgets are double-voltage, you just need a fitting connector. In the event that they are not double voltage, you will require both a fitting connector and a voltage converter.

Using   Gadgets   Safely:

To try not to harm your electronic gadgets, try to

utilize them with the right voltage and attachment connectors.

Assuming you're uncertain about the voltage prerequisites of your gadgets, actually look at the name or counsel the producer's determinations prior to connecting them.

By monitoring Ireland's power norms and utilizing the fitting attachment connectors, you can securely utilize your electronic gadgets during your outing.

Chapter 11: Food

Traditional Irish dishes and specialties

Customary Irish food is generous, soothing, and well established in the nation's set of experiences and culture. While current Irish cooking has developed to incorporate various worldwide impacts, there are a few conventional dishes and claims to fame that stay famous in Ireland. Here is an extensive manual for conventional Irish dishes and strengths:

Irish   Stew:
Irish stew is a good dish made with sheep or lamb, potatoes, onions, and carrots. It is slow-cooked to soften the meat and foster rich flavors. A few varieties likewise incorporate different vegetables, like parsnips and turnips.

Colcannon:
Colcannon is a conventional Irish dish made with

pureed potatoes and either cabbage or kale, blended in with spread, milk, and now and then scallions or leeks. It is often filled in as a side dish with meat or as a primary course.

Boxty:

Boxty is a customary Irish potato hotcake made with ground potatoes, flour, baking powder, and buttermilk or milk. It is seared until fresh and brilliant brown and can be filled in as a side dish or a fundamental course with fixings like sharp cream and smoked salmon.

Coddle:

Pamper is a customary Irish dish made with wieners, bacon, onions, and potatoes, slow-cooked in a stock or stock. A good and encouraging dish is often served on cool, cold days.

Irish Soft Drink Bread:

Irish soft drink bread is a customary Irish bread made with flour, baking soda, salt, and buttermilk. It is a speedy and simple bread to make, with a thick surface and a marginally tart flavor. It is frequently presented with margarine and jam.

"Guinness Hamburger Stew":

Guinness hamburger stew is a generous and delightful dish made with meat, onions, carrots, and potatoes, slow-cooked in a stock made with Guinness bold brew. The brew adds a rich, malty flavor to the stew.

Barmbrack:

Barmbrack is a customary Irish nut cake made with dried natural products, flavors, and now and then bourbon or tea. It is frequently served cut and buttered, particularly around Halloween, when it is accepted to have fortune-telling properties.

Seafood Chowder:

- Ireland's waterfront area implies that fish is a famous fixing in numerous customary dishes. Fish chowder is a rich soup made with an assortment of fish, like fish, mussels, and prawns, alongside potatoes, onions, and spices.

Irish Breakfast:

A customary Irish breakfast is a generous feast that ordinarily incorporates bacon, frankfurters, highly contrasting pudding, eggs, tomatoes, mushrooms, and toast. A significant dinner is, in many cases, served at extraordinary events or as an end-of-week treat.

Apple   Crumble:

Apple disintegrate is an exemplary treat made with stewed apples finished off with a brittle combination of flour, margarine, sugar, and oats. It is heated until brilliant and served warm with custard or cream.

These are only a couple of instances of conventional Irish dishes and claims to fame that exhibit the rich and various culinary legacies of Ireland. Whether you're testing these dishes in a neighborhood bar or taking a shot at cooking them yourself, conventional Irish food is certain to please your taste buds and warm your spirit.

Best places to try local cuisine

Ireland is famous for its generous and delightful food, and there are a lot of spots throughout the nation where you can test conventional Irish dishes and strengths. From comfortable bars to top-notch cafés, here are the absolute best places to attempt neighborhood cooking in Ireland:

Dublin:

Dublin is home to a large number of cafés and restaurants where you can try customary Irish food. The city's bars are an extraordinary spot to begin, with many good dishes like Irish stew, fried fish and French fries, and meat and Guinness pie.

For a more upscale eating experience, make a beeline for one of Dublin's fancy cafés, where you can test current translations of conventional Irish dishes utilizing privately obtained fixings.

Galway:

Galway is known for its energetic food scene, with a lot of cafés and bistros presenting heavenly neighborhood cooking. The city's fish is especially eminent, with dishes like, for example, fish chowder and Galway clams being famous decisions.

The city's clamoring market, the Galway Market, is likewise an extraordinary spot to test nearby produce and distinctive food varieties, including cheeses, breads, and meats.

Cork:

Stopper is a food darling's heaven, with plenty of cafés, bistros, and food markets offering an extensive variety of neighborhood and worldwide cooking. The English Market in Stopper City is a must-visit. It slows down selling new produce, meats, and cheeses, and that's only the tip of the iceberg.

The city's bars are likewise an incredible spot to test customary Irish dishes, with many contributing unrecorded music and a warm, inviting air.

Belfast:

Belfast has a flourishing food scene, with a blend of conventional and present-day cafés presenting scrumptious nearby cooking. The city's bars are an extraordinary spot to attempt customary Irish dishes like Irish stew, boxty, and soft drink bread.

The St. George's Market in Belfast is likewise a must-visit, with an extensive variety of food slow-downs offering everything from neighborhood fish to global cooking.

Rural   Areas:

The absolute best places to attempt neighborhood cooking in Ireland are in the country's provincial regions, where you'll find conventional bars and eateries presenting good dishes made with privately obtained fixings.

Province Kerry, District Donegal, and Region Mayo are especially eminent for their customary Irish food, with numerous cafés and restaurants offering dishes that feature the best of neighborhood produce.

By and large, Ireland offers an abundance of chances to test customary Irish food, from comfortable bars to high-end cafés. Whether you're in Dublin, Galway, Plug, Belfast, or a rustic region, you're certain to find flavorful neighborhood dishes that will tempt your taste buds and provide you with a genuine taste of Ireland.

Vegetarian and vegan options

Ireland's culinary scene has developed to take care of a large number of dietary inclinations, including veggie lovers and vegetarians who eat fewer carbs. While customary Irish food is frequently revolved around meat and dairy items, there are a lot of cafés and restaurants the nation over that offer flavorful vegan and vegetarian choices. Here is an exhaustive manual for veggie lovers and vegetarian choices in Ireland:

Vegetarian   Options:
Vegan choices are generally accessible in Ireland, with numerous eateries offering non-meat versions of customary dishes. Famous vegan dishes incorporate vegetable stew, veggie shepherd's pie, and vegetable curry.
Most cafés in Ireland are glad to oblige vegan demands, and many have committed veggie lover

menus or obviously stamped vegan choices on their menus.

Vegan   Options:

Vegetarian choices are likewise turning out to be more pervasive in Ireland, with numerous cafés offering veggie-loving forms of customary dishes. Famous veggie lover dishes incorporate vegetarian shepherd's pie, veggie lover curry, and veggie lover burgers.

Numerous cafés in Ireland currently offer devoted veggie lover menus or obviously stamped vegetarian choices on their menus. A few eateries even spend significant time on vegetarian cooking, offering an extensive variety of plant-based dishes.

Specialty Bistros and Restaurants:

There are a few specialty bistros and eateries in Ireland that cater explicitly to veggie lovers and vegetarians. These foundations offer an extensive variety of plant-based dishes, including plates of mixed greens, wraps, sandwiches, and treats.

These bistros and cafés frequently utilize privately obtained, natural fixings to make heavenly and nutritious dinners that are reasonable for veggie lovers and vegetarians alike.

Ethnic Cuisine:

Ethnic cafés in Ireland, for example, Indian, Center Eastern, and Asian eateries, frequently have a large number of vegetarian and vegan choices on their menus. These cooking styles generally utilize various flavors and fixings that are normally veggie lovers and vegetarian cordial.

These cafés are an extraordinary choice for veggie lovers and vegetarians searching for delightful and various eating choices in Ireland.

Farmers' Business Sectors and Food Festivals:

Ranchers' business sectors and food celebrations in Ireland are extraordinary spots to track down new, privately obtained veggie lovers and vegetarian food. Numerous merchants in these business sectors offer an assortment of plant-based dishes, tidbits, and fixings.

These business sectors and celebrations frequently highlight cooking exhibits and tastings, offering you the chance to test an extensive variety of veggie-loving and vegetarian dishes.

Supermarkets and Wellbeing Food Stores: General stores and wellbeing food stores in Ireland offer a great many veggie-lovers and vegetarian items, including meat substitutes, dairy cheeses, and plant-based milks.

These stores likewise stock different new leafy foods, grains, vegetables, and nuts, making it simple to make delightful veggie and vegetarian dinners at home.

Generally, Ireland offers a different and invigorating scope of veggie lovers and vegetarian choices for explorers and local people alike. Whether you're searching for customary Irish dishes with a plant-based curve or global cooking that is totally meat and sans dairy, you're certain to track down a lot of delectable choices to suit your preferences.

Dining etiquette in Ireland

Feasting manners in Ireland is like that in numerous Western nations, with a couple of one-of-a-kind traditions and customs. Whether you're eating in a café or a private home, it's essential to notice these behavior rules to guarantee a lovely feasting experience. Here is an extensive manual for eating manners in Ireland:

Making Reservations:

It's prudent to reserve a spot, particularly at famous cafés or during active times, to keep away from dissatisfaction.

While reserving a spot, make certain to determine any dietary limitations or unique requests you might have.

Arrival and Seating:

Show up on time for your booking, or call ahead on the off chance that you will be late.

In a café, stand by to be situated by the host or leader. In a confidential home, stand by to be coordinated to your seat by your host.

Table Manners:

Hold on until everybody at the table has been served prior to starting to eat.

Keep your elbows off the table and your mind in your lap while not eating.

Bite with your mouth shut and try not to converse

with food in your mouth. Use utensils from an external perspective, beginning with the chilled fork and blade and working in your direction toward the primary course utensils.

Toasting:

Toasting is a typical practice in Ireland, particularly during celebratory feasts or get-togethers.

At the point when somebody offers a toast, it's standard to raise your glass, visually connect, and take a taste of your beverage. You may likewise give your very own toast as a trade-off.

Paying the Bill:

In eateries, the bill is commonly offered and would be useful when you're done eating. It's standard to share the bill uniformly among coffee shops, although one individual might propose to pay for the whole dinner.

Assuming that you're a respectable visitor, it's acceptable to propose to pay for the feast, yet your host might demand payment.

Tipping:

Tipping is standard in Ireland, and a tip of 10-15% is standard in cafés.

A few eateries might incorporate a help charge on the bill, so make certain to check prior to leaving an extra tip.

Special Considerations:

In the event that you're eating in a confidential home, bringing a little gift for your host, for example, a container of wine or a crate of chocolates, is standard.

In the event that you have dietary limitations or inclinations, let your host or server in ahead of time so they can oblige you.

By noticing these eating decorum rules, you can partake in a wonderful and deferential feasting experience in Ireland. Whether you're eating in a café or a private home, these traditions and customs will assist you with exploring the feasting scene with ease and effortlessness.

Chapter 12: Conclusion

Final tips and recommendations for a memorable trip to Ireland

An excursion to Ireland guarantees shocking scenes, rich history, and warm cordiality. To capitalize on your visit and guarantee an important encounter, think about these last tips and suggestions:

Weather   Preparedness:
Ireland's weather conditions can be capricious, so pack layers and waterproof apparel. Be ready for downpours whenever, even in the summer, and bring an umbrella or waterproof shell.

Travel   Insurance:
Think about buying head-out protection to cover any unforeseen occasions, like excursion abrogations or health-related crises.

Currency:

Ireland utilizes the euro (€). It's fitting to have some money close by for little buys, as not all spots acknowledge credit or check cards.

Driving:

Assuming you intend to drive in Ireland, get to know the nearby traffic rules and guidelines.

Make sure to drive on the left half of the street, and be careful on limited, winding streets.

Safety:

Ireland is by and large a protected objective, yet practicing alertness, particularly in packed tourist areas, is dependably shrewd.

Watch out for your things and know about your environmental elements.

Health:

Ireland has brilliant medical services offices, yet having travel protection if there should arise an occurrence of health-related emergencies is fitting.

Know about any wellbeing warnings or inoculations expected prior to venturing out to Ireland.

Local Customs:

really get to know nearby traditions and decorum, particularly while visiting strict destinations or connecting with local people.

Regard neighborhood customs and practices, and dress humbly while visiting houses of worship or strict locales.

Tipping:

Tipping is valued but not generally anticipated in Ireland. It's standard to leave a 10-15% tip in cafés on the off chance that the help was great.

9. WiFi and Connectivity:

Wi-Fi is broadly accessible in lodgings, bistros, and eateries in Ireland. Consider buying a nearby SIM card for portable information if necessary.

Explore Past the Cities:

While Dublin, Galway, Stopper, and Belfast are must-visit urban communities, don't pass up Ireland's shockingly open country and beachfront regions.

Investigate the Wild Atlantic Way, visit the Bluffs of Moher, and find the magnificence of the Ring of Kerry.

Immerse Yourself in Irish Culture:

Experience customary Irish music and dance at nearby bars and widespread developments.

Visit exhibition halls, displays, and memorable locales to find out about Ireland's rich history and legacy.

Be Open to New Experiences:

Ireland is loaded with shocks, so be open to attempting new food varieties, meeting new individuals, and investigating in an unexpected direction.

Embrace the Irish soul of neighborliness and partake in the glow and amiability of local people.

An outing to Ireland is certain to be a critical encounter loaded with stunning landscapes, interesting history, and warm neighborliness. By following these tips and proposals, you can take advantage of your visit and make enduring memories in the Emerald Isle.

Additional Resources and Websites for further Information

For additional data and assets to assist with arranging your outing to Ireland, think about the following:

Tourism Ireland (www.ireland.com): The authority is the travel industry site for Ireland, offering data on attractions, facilities, and occasions, and that's just the beginning. gives travel tips, proposed schedules, and commonsense data for guests.

Failte Ireland (www.failte ireland.ie): The public is the travel industry advancement expert for Ireland, offering data on travel industry drives, occasions, and attractions. gives assets to organizations in the travel industry and makes advances manageable as the industry rehearses.

Discover Ireland Centers:
- Situated all through Ireland, these guest places offer data, guides, and advisers to assist you with arranging your outing. staffed by learned local people who can give customized suggestions and counsel.

Irish Vacationer Help Service (www.itas.ie): gives help and backing to vacationers who have been casualties of wrongdoing or who need assistance during their visit to Ireland. offers a 24-hour helpline and helps with revealing violations to the police.

5. Irish Vehicle Rentals (www.irishcarrentals.com): offers vehicle rental services in Ireland, with a large number of vehicles accessible. gives data on driving in Ireland, including street rules, protection, and security tips.

Irish Ferries (www.irish ferries.com): offers ship administrations between Ireland, the UK, and France, permitting you to investigate a greater amount of Europe during your excursion. gives data on ship courses, timetables, and charges.

Irish Rail (www.irish rail.ie): the public rail line organization in Ireland, offering train administrations all through the country. gives data on train courses, timetables, and passages, as well as movement passes for travelers.

Bus Eireann (www.buseireann.ie): the public transport organization in Ireland, offering transport administrations all through the country. gives data on transport courses, timetables, and passages, as well as movement passes for sightseers.

Heritage Ireland (www.heritage ireland.ie): oversees and works on a scope of legacy locales and attractions in Ireland, including palaces, galleries, and archeological destinations. gives data on opening times, affirmation costs, and unique occasions at legacy locales.

Wild Atlantic Way (www.wild atlantic way.com): offers data on Ireland's seaside driving course, which extends north of 2,500 km along the west shoreline of Ireland.

gives maps, recommended agendas, and data on attractions along the course.

These assets and sites can provide significant data and help you plan your trip to Ireland. Whether you're searching for movement tips, convenience choices, or data on attractions, these assets can assist you with taking advantage of your visit to the Emerald Isle.

Feedback and suggestions for improving the guide

Criticism and ideas are significant in further developing any movement guide, and your feedback is enormously valuable. Here are some ways to upgrade this manual to make it more helpful for future explorers:

Interactive   Maps:
Adding intelligent guides to the side could assist users with picturing the areas of attractions, facilities,   and   different   focal   points.

These guides could be interactive, giving more data about every area when chosen.

User Audits and Ratings:
Consolidating client surveys and evaluations for attractions, facilities, and eateries could provide significant bits of knowledge to users. This element could assist perusers with pursuing informed choices in light of the encounters of different voyagers.

Local Insights:
Counting tips and bits of knowledge from local people could upgrade the aide's legitimacy and give one-of-a-kind points of view. Local people could contribute suggestions for unexpected yet invaluable treasures, less popular attractions, and encounters outside of what might be expected.

Seasonal Recommendations:
Giving occasional proposals for exercises, occasions, and attractions could assist voyagers with arranging their excursions all the more. This could include data for occasional

celebrations, climate contemplations, and the best times to visit specific attractions.

Budget-Accommodation Options:

Including more data-driven spending plans with amicable choices for facilities, feasting, and exercises could help frugal voyagers.

This could incorporate suggestions for reasonable inns, lodgings, and diners, as well as free or minimal-cost exercises.

Accessibility Information:

Remembering data for availability highlights at attractions, facilities, and eateries could assist voyagers with portability issues or incapacities.

This could include subtleties for wheelchair access, open bathrooms, and different offices.

Cultural Etiquette:

Giving more point-by-point data on social manners and customs could assist voyagers with exploring social circumstances all the more certainly.

This could include tips for good manners, eating manners, and deferential conduct in various settings.

Environmental Sustainability:

Integrating data on earth-supportable practices and eco-accommodating choices could speak to naturally cognizant voyagers.

This could incorporate proposals for eco-accommodating facilities, transportation choices, and exercises.

Interactive Schedule Planner:

Counting an intelligent agenda organizer could assist perusers with arranging their excursions all the more proficiently.

This component could permit clients to choose attractions, facilities, and exercises and create a customized schedule.

Language Support:

Giving language backing to non-English speakers could make the aid more open to a more extensive crowd.

This could incorporate interpretations of key data into various dialects.

Your criticism and ideas are significant in working on this aid. By consolidating these thoughts, we can make a more thorough and easy-to-understand asset for explorers arranging an outing to Ireland.